A Cape Cod Girl's Life Adventure

by Pearl Marion (Marney) Williams

Edited by David W. Williams

ISBN-13: 978-1-7344338-4-5

Font: Candara

Cover photos:

Pearl with her older sister Pauline in family car
Sagamore Bridge 2017, taken by Kevin F. Williams

Previous books:

The Adventures and Philosophies of an Old Lady, 1996
Library of Congress Catalog Card Number 96-94675

Conclusion to the Adventures and Philosophies of an Old Lady, 2003

Foreword

My mother wrote two autobiographical books: The Adventures and Philosophies of an Old Lady (1996) and Conclusion to The Adventures and Philosophies of an Old Lady (2003). These printings were relatively short booklets and made primarily for family and close friends. The family has decided to combine both booklets and self-publish them in this hardback book version emphasizing her Cape Cod roots. We believe that there is an historical context where her general memories and struggles growing up and growing old as part of the WW2 generation in 20th century America deserve to be made accessible to future generations.

Every intent has been made to honor Pearl's wishes that her words and grammar remain exactly as written. But, realistically, there's not an author alive who wouldn't benefit from (and usually gets) a good edit review. The human brain has a way of filling in blanks or changing letters to correct words on the fly. A second, less subjective, brain has a much better chance of catching those last few discrepancies. That said, a very few non contextual edits were made—for clarity and organization mainly. Where she included family pictures, we have added family members that joined us after she finished her last writings in 1996, then 2003. Pearl has a colloquial style that is honest and satisfying, and we wanted desperately to keep her flavor. She wrote as she spoke, and you will feel as though Pearl is talking to you as you read her words in describing what it was like living in America from 1927 to 2003.

Because she would live on until 2010, for completeness an afterword has been added with some commentary on the remainder of her life—and that of her husband Howard's life as well. This was pulled from an autobiographical book I had self-published through Ingram Spark and Amazon in 2019: A Baby Boomer's Unexamined Life. In this, I give my take on the Williams/Marney family; Cape Cod, New England, and Florida; growing up and growing old; and a perspective on life and the changing society from a baby boomer's perspective.

Also included in the afterword are numerous remembrances and well wishes in a "This is your life" manner that were written to Pearl and Howard on the occasion of their 50th wedding anniversary by family and close friends. The book closes with the obituaries for Howard in 2013 and Pearl in 2010, and their joint Memorial Service that was held on June 29, 2013 in Osterville.

I have enjoyed this re-release of my mother's writings. I feel as though I've met my parents all over again.

David W. Williams / Son number 3 of 5
March 31, 2020

Table of Contents

[Original Cover]

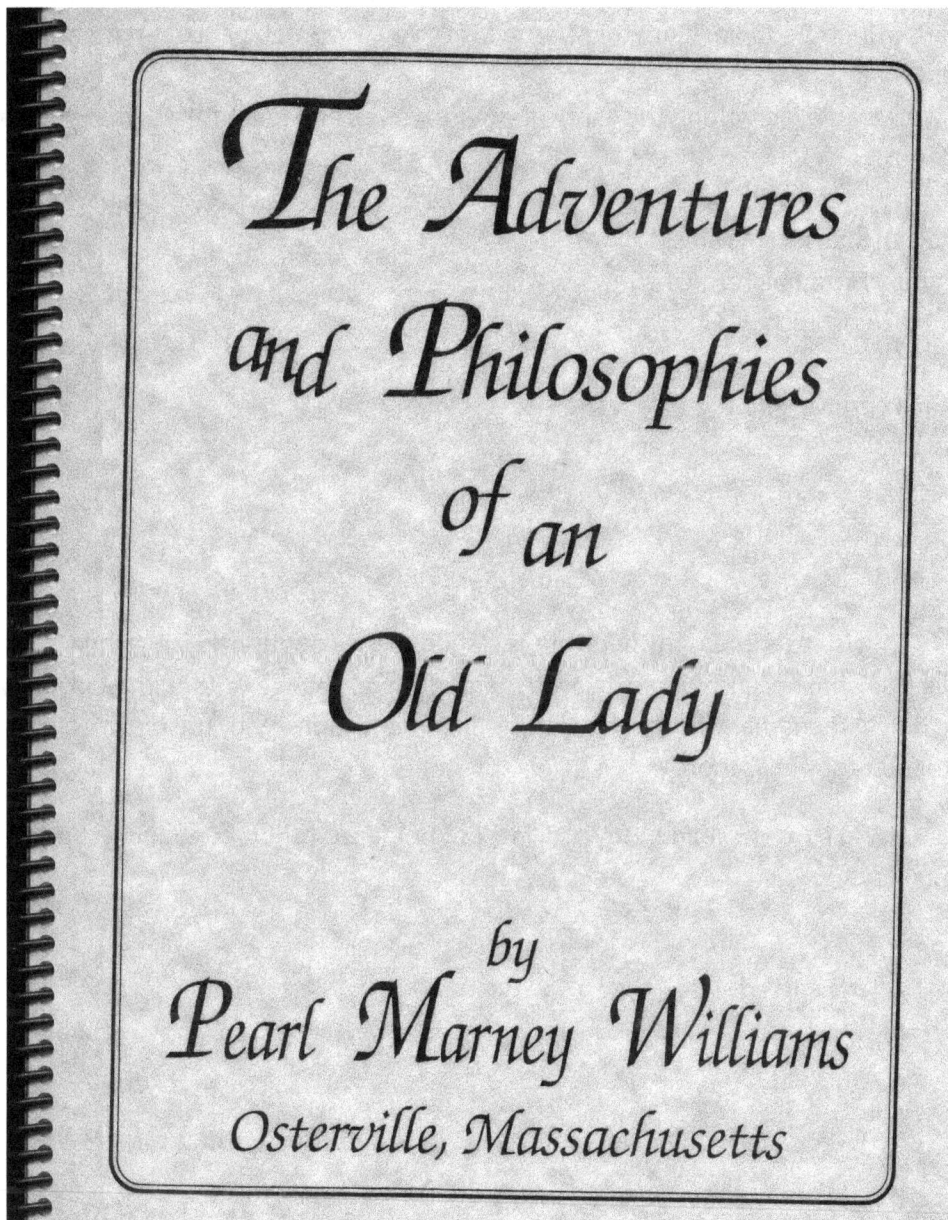

The Adventures and Philosophies of an Old Lady

by

Pearl Marney Williams
Osterville, Massachusetts

Library of Congress Catalog Card Number 96-94675

Dedication

This book is dedicated to the ones I love, my children and their families, and especially to my son, Kevin, who talked me into writing this book.

One day several months ago, I was telling him about something that happened, or something that was said, when my mother was alive. He said, "Write that down, Mom, write that down. If anything happens to you, I won't be able to remember all these things."

I have enjoyed writing this story of my life, Kevin, and hope this is what you had in mind.

Pearl Marney Williams
4939 Floramar Terrace #607
New Port Richey, Florida 34652

16 February 1996

Appreciation

I wish to express my deep appreciation to my daughter-in-law, Linda Williams, who, because of my delayed memories and change of thoughts on many occasions, spent many hours putting this document, along with the pictures, into the computer for publication.

And to my husband, Howard, last but not least, for his continuing support in many ways.

My Childhood Years

Now that I am old and ailing, and have lots of time to think, fond memories keep appearing and lingering in my daydreams. Little incidents I had long forgotten about now appear quite clear.

When I think back on my childhood now, I realize what an enchanted life I lived. I was born in Fairhaven, Massachusetts, on 9 March 1927, the daughter of Fraser A. and Martha O. Marney. My mother said I was a very easy birth. When I had chicken pox, I only had two pox. When I had whooping cough, I only whooped once!

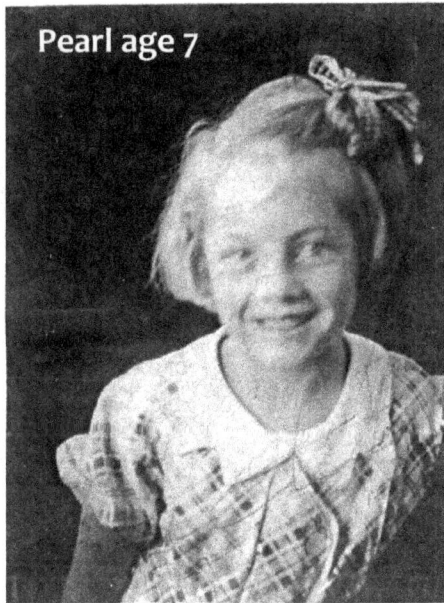

Pearl age 7

I had a sister, Polly (Pauline), who was five years older than I. She had chicken pox before me and she was completely covered. And when she had the whooping cough, she almost died! Her life was completely different from mine. When she was three, she fell out of a three-story tenement apartment in Fairhaven. My mother said it had rained the night before, so she did not get hurt. When she was two, her dress caught on the tea kettle on one of those old black stoves. She fell over and her back and legs were very badly scalded. My mother said she was petrified. She wrapped my sister in a sheet and sent for the doctor. When he arrived she went and hid in a closet. The Doctor treated the wounds, but did not take her to the hospital. He came every day and every day my mother took her to the ocean and let the salt air blow on the wounds. The Doctor told my mother that was what saved her life. To the day she died, she had deep scars on her back and parts of her legs.

My Childhood Years

While living in Fairhaven, a few years after Polly was born, my mother got sick. The Doctor finally determined she had appendicitis. He told her she must go to the hospital but my mother did not want to go. The next day he came back. The pain was all gone, but she had a fever. The Doctor told her that her appendix had ruptured and that if she did not go to the hospital, she would die. Consequently she went to the hospital. They determined that she had peritonitis, and they had to remove one ovary. She said she had tubes sticking in her all over the place, and was in the hospital a long time. They told her she would never have any more children!!

After I was born they told her she could only have GIRLS! In time I had four more siblings—All BOYS! Osborne, Edison, Arthur and Kenneth. So my mother surely had her hands full trying to care for all of us.

Now that reminds me of a story my mother once told me. She said there was a Mrs. McGillicutty in town. She thought she was pregnant, and went to the Doctor. He said, "Oh, no, Mrs. McGillicutty, you are not pregnant. What you are feeling is gas." A few months later Mrs. McGillicutty decided to go to a different doctor. Nine months later Mrs. McGillicutty was out walking her baby when the first doctor came along. He said, "Oh, my, my, Mrs. McGillicutty, what do we have here?" She said, "Oh, it's really nothing, Doctor; just a little fart with a bonnet on it!"

One and a half years after me, my brother Obbie was born. He was just a baby, only a few months old, when we moved to Osterville, Massachusetts. My father was a carpenter and he was offered a job building the old Osterville Schoolhouse on West Bay Road. We rented a house on Pond Street belonging to Ed Harvey Lewis, now lived in and owned by Jesse Stringer. I remember we did not have a bathroom. There was an outhouse, and I remember the old Sears Roebuck catalog was always needed to complete the job. [Talk about free advertising.]

After the Osterville schoolhouse was completed, my father went to work for Daniel Brothers as a carpenter, until he died of a heart attack in 1956. (This business was later bought and run by my brother, Obbie, and John Lahteine, and was known as Marney and Lahteine, Inc.)

My father was a very hard worker. We had only lived on Pond Street a couple of years before my father, on one of our walks through the woods, discovered the house that we eventually purchased. It was on an old dirt road between Joshua's Pond and Sam's Pond; the address was called Off Pond Street. He paid $1,800.00 for it. The street is now extended and renamed Tower Hill Road. I was probably about 4 or 5 years old at the time of purchase but I can still remember peeking in through the windows. It had an old black stove, an old black sink, a well for water, and a ladder in the dining room leading up to the unfinished attic loft where there was additional room for sleeping.

My father spent most of his spare time working on the house after we bought it. He put in dormers (both front and back), a porch, built a garage, and even enlarged the foundation to a full foundation under the house, all by himself. When we moved in, the house only had an 8 ft by 8 ft space under the kitchen, made with rocks, where the fusebox was kept. Every once in a while the lights would go out and, if he didn't have a fuse, he would put a penny in behind the fuse to make the lights go back on.

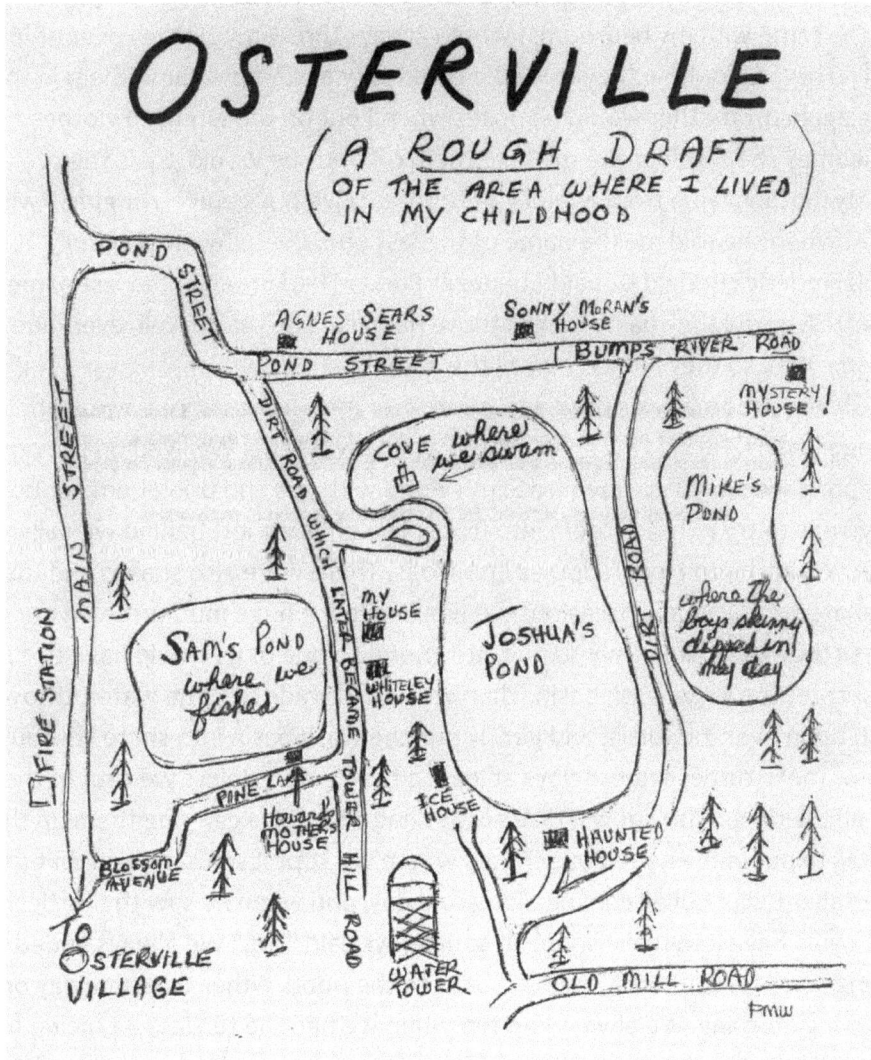

OSTERVILLE

(A ROUGH DRAFT OF THE AREA WHERE I LIVED IN MY CHILDHOOD)

POND STREET

AGNES SEARS HOUSE

SONNY MORAN'S HOUSE

POND STREET

BUMPS RIVER ROAD

MYSTERY HOUSE !

MAIN STREET

FIRE STATION

DIRT ROAD WHICH LATER BECAME TOWER HILL ROAD

COVE where we swam

MIKE'S POND

where the boys skinny dipped in my day

SAM'S POND where we fished

MY HOUSE

WHITELEY HOUSE

JOSHUA'S POND

DIRT ROAD

PINE LANE

Howard Mothers HOUSE

ICE HOUSE

HAUNTED HOUSE

BLOSSOM AVENUE

TO OSTERVILLE VILLAGE

WATER TOWER

HILL ROAD

OLD MILL ROAD

PMW

One thing the original house did have was a bathroom! However, because of the clay-like soil, it seemed as though it was always plugged up. Once again it was back to the old outhouse. I can remember late at night, sometimes, in the middle of winter when it was bitter cold and there was snow on the ground, we would have to put on our winter coats and boots and scarves to make the trek out. My poor mother would always bundle up and go out with me when I was little.

I can honestly say that I had one of the best and kindest mothers anyone could hope for. When I think back now, I feel so guilty that I did not do more for both of my parents to help make their lives more pleasant. I can remember coming home from school in the rain and throwing my old wet coat on the wringer washing machine in the kitchen. It would invariably fall on the floor, and my mother would be so upset the next day when I put the old wrinkled coat on to go to school.

The same with my bedroom; I would always throw my clothes over or into a chair with no regard for how they looked. I could very easily have hung them in the closet. Once again my mother would be upset when I put on the wrinkled clothes. Sometimes she would make me take them off and she would press them.

My mother came from a family of thirteen: Five boys and eight girls. I will never forget when she told me the name of the last one, the baby of the family. It was Ralph Frederick Ronald Donald Ebenezer Parker (Parker being the last name). I said to her, "Why did they name him all those names?" She said, "Well, everyone wanted to name him, so they named him all the names."

Obbie (Osborne) was the next in line after me. He was about a year and one half younger than I. He was my greatest pal when I was little. We lived on the ponds. In the spring we would go down to Sam's Pond with jars and bring home gobs of jellied pollywogs to try to hatch them into frogs. The ones we left behind we daily watched grow tails and turn from tadpoles into frogs. There were also snakes and turtles that fascinated us. On many occasions we would catch a huge mud turtle on our lines. Of course they were too heavy to pull into shore, so one of us would have to run up the hill and get the large wash basin. Then we would wade into the water, throw the wash basin over the turtle, and gently pull the wash basin into shore without getting bitten. These turtles were always at least a foot wide. (Unless we caught the same one all the time. Who knows?) We always had a struggle carrying them up the hill by the tail to put in the hen-house. That's where we kept it so that it couldn't get away. I remember Bullet Lovell coming along one day, and when he saw the turtle, he asked if he could have it to make soup. Of course, we said "No." We always ended up feeling sorry for the turtle, taking it back to the pond, either the same day or the following morning. We always had fun when we had the turtles — putting food in front of their mouths and trying to get them to eat. It was also exciting when we returned them to the pond and seeing them swim away!

MY MOTHER'S FAMILY (The Charles E. Parker Family)

Standing: Alice Miriam, Harry Freeman, Frank Newton, Shepard John, Rainsford Charles, Kate Vera. Seated: Helen Vera, Charles Edward (my grandfather) holding baby Ralph Frederick Ronald Donald Ebenezer, Martha Dorcas Fox (my grandmother), Laura May. Front; Dorothy Ada, Martha Olive (my mother), Hazel Maus, Celista Eileen.

My good father

My sweet mother

There was only one other house near us at this location between the ponds. The Elmer Whiteleys were our neighbors. They had five children, but Pat and Beverley were the oldest and closest to Obbie and my ages. They were our pals and enjoyed many of our adventures with us.

We spent many an hour at Sam's Pond during the summer, and when we weren't there, we were at Joshua's swimming. We all learned to swim at an early age; Polly taught me how. There was always a raft at Joshua's with a diving board. We were always swimming from one side of the pond [cove] to the other, or throwing rocks from the diving board and diving for them.

I can remember one time before I had learned to swim when my sister pushed me all over the pond on a railroad tie. When we returned to the cove from which we had started, and she was pushing me into shore, she said, "Can you stand yet?" With that I hopped off the railroad tie into the water, which was about six inches over my head! I can remember standing there on the bottom of the pond with my face all scrunched up, crying and gulping down gobs of water. Before long my sister grabbed me under the arms and pulled me out. I sat on the bank a long time after that with a towel wrapped around me, chilled and water-logged!

We always took ivory soap and a wash rag with us to the pond where we had a bath and washed our hair! When I think back now on "wash rag," it sounds so funny. But I'm sure we didn't buy face cloths in those days. We always ripped an old towel into pieces for wash rags!

Joshua's Pond, where we swam.

We lived a very sheltered life when we were little. So much so that the only one to make it through first grade without staying back was Polly. All the rest of us, I and my four brothers, all stayed back in the first grade. [Note: Pearl graduated HS when she was 18, on schedule, so her parents must have enrolled her (and her brothers?) a year ahead of time.] I can remember one continuous crying jag. Every day my sister would take me to school, and the minute she would leave me, I would start to cry. They tried everything to stop me from crying. Just about every day, they would take me in to sit beside Polly in the fifth grade until I stopped crying. I can remember Miss Temple paddling my rear end. (That didn't do any good.) My mother would give Polly two cents every day to buy penny candy at the News Stand to get me to go to school. I was fine until the candy was gone, and then I would start to cry. Finally the school told my mother that, if I didn't stop crying, I would have to stay home. That night my mother gave me a good lecture. I don't remember what she said, but the crying ceased! However I did have to repeat the year!

Sept 2, 1940? Sam's Pond, where we fished.

In those days, if you were not six before January lst, you had to take a test. I can remember taking the test. Some of the things I remember I had to do were open the window, close the door, tie my shoe, and pick a quarter out of some money! I passed the test!

Polly, Obbie, Ed, Art, Kenny and I would all attend the Osterville School on West Bay Road, which my father helped build. It was a fun school to attend. Lida Sherman was Principal and Virginia Adams and Jeanette Fraser, both Osterville residents, were teachers.

My Childhood Years

I wasn't always an angel though. When I was in the third grade, the teacher went out of the room. I don't know how it happened, but some of the other kids dared me to jump out of the second-story window! Of course, I jumped! The teacher was coming down the hall and caught me coming in the outside door. She said I was to stay after school, and she would have to "strap" me. I was really scared. That afternoon, right after school, I went up and told the teacher that I had to go home because we had company (which we didn't!) She gave me a lecture and said I could have broken my leg, and let me go.

We always had "special" days that we looked forward to at the good old Osterville School. Every year before the school closed for the summer, the whole school would go on a picnic to Parker's River in Yarmouth. It would take several school buses to pick us all up at the school and return us mid-afternoon. We would all take a bag lunch, but we could buy incidentals (Potato Chips, drinks, etc.) there, too. There were many showers in amongst the trees to rinse off with after we swam in the river. I have often wondered if it is still there. We have never been able to find it since, especially so many years later.

We also always celebrated Memorial Day with a parade to the memorial in front of the Kalas Country Store, where we had so much fun buying "penny" candy. We all had to bring wild flowers to the school that day and then we marched from the school to the memorial and then, after the service, we marched to the cemetery to put the flowers on any grave that had a flag on it. The service always ended before lunch that day, and we always ran home for our first swim of the year in Joshua's Pond. The water was always ice cold, but we ran in anyway - and then we had to stay in the water to keep warm! (Today, you can't even do that!)

We always exchanged Valentine cards on Valentine's Day and we also had an Easter Egg hunt in the school yard each year at Easter. They threw paper eggs in various colors over the grounds, with some marked for prizes.

At Christmas time, we drew names and exchanged gifts. I remember one year that a member of my family had someone draw his name by someone who we thought would give him a really nice gift! We were all so excited! ------- He got a stick of gum!!

Another thing I remember was that they sold milk in school those days, paid for by the week and delivered mid morning each day. It cost 1 penny for a small carton of white milk and 2 pennys for a carton of chocolate milk. Every time Buddy Scudder was out sick, they would give me his chocolate milk! I guess they thought I was not getting enough to eat or something, because we were all thin in those days! (Don't we wish it now!)

In those days nobody gave a thought to pollution. The water in the ponds was so crystal clear. In the winter when the ice would freeze over, we would lie on the ice and watch all the fish swimming around below. We would make a hole in the ice when we were thirsty to get a drink of water.

Sam's pond was always one of the first to freeze over. The climate of the Cape in those days was a lot different from what it is now. It was very cold during the winter, and we always had lots of snow. Today it is very mild. In those days it wasn't anything to have a three-foot high snow storm. I can remember the snow being over our heads!

January and February were always great skating months. When we weren't sliding down the hill to Sam's Pond, we were skating. When it snowed, the older boys were always right there to clear the ice. They always cleared a patch for skating—and a patch for ice hockey! The older boys always had bonfires on the edge of the pond. Sometimes they brought tires to burn. And sometimes we would bring marshmallows to cook. When we got tired skating, we would go sit by the fire to get warm.

One of the most dangerous things we ever did, I guess, was when we skated on the ice before it was really solid. The young folks would form a long line holding hands, which we called the "whip." We would all skate as fast as we could, and then the first person would come to a stop, leaving the rest of the line to swing around. The ice had sort of a ripple effect beneath our skates. We called it a bend-e-go. I can remember I was on the end of the line one time when the force was so fierce that I lost my balance. I slipped sideways on the ice and hurt my hip. I turned deathly ill and thought for sure my hip was broken. I laid there until the sickening feeling went away. Then I went and sat by the fire until I recovered.

Joshua's Pond always froze over later. It was a larger pond and took longer to freeze. So it was probably February before we transferred from Sam's to Joshua's to skate. Jesse Murray had an ice house on one end of Joshua's. Every year they would cut large chunks of ice out of the pond and store it in the ice house in sawdust for delivery to the area residents for their ice boxes. I watched them take it out one day, and they were huge pieces. I'll bet they were 14" thick!

Oh, yes, and what would a childhood be without a haunted house? Well, we had one of those, too. It was located on one end of Joshua's Pond—over near the ice house. The grass grew high and the wild flowers and bushes grew in abundance around it. With a tree here and there, the house itself looked as though it hadn't been lived in for years!! It was all rotting away. Every once in a while, Obbie, Pat, Beverley and I would trudge over there and go through it. The floors would groan and creak. (I don't think the houses in those days ever did have much of a foundation.) It's a wonder we didn't fall through. It is also a miracle that we didn't fall into the well. It was only partially covered and looked to be VERY deep. We kids were really scared when we went through the house, but that didn't stop us any from going over there. We often speculated who lived there and wondered what ever happened to them?!! It has all rotted away now and trees have taken its place.

On the way back we would sometimes stop at the ice house, where Jesse Murray kept the ice, and jump in the sawdust. I don't think anybody ever knew we did that!

Now I must tell you about another house which was out on Bumps River Road. We always peeked in the windows every year when we went blueberrying out in that area. The table was always set as though somebody was expecting to eat soon, but nobody ever lived there!! The rumor around town was that a couple had lived there. They went horseback riding around the ponds early one evening and never returned. It was thought that they got into some quicksand in one of the swamps - AND DISAPPEARED!!!

Oh, we had such a great time when we were young! Christmas was always such a joyous time of year. Believing in Santa Claus was always so exciting. We started writing notes to Santa right after Thanksgiving. The back of the chimney in our house extended from the living room into the dining room. The fireplace was in the living room. The part in the dining room which was enclosed had a small door halfway up the wall which, when open, exposed the back of the chimney. That's where we use to throw our notes to Santa.

Every once in a while my mother would stick her head in there and start screeching. She would say the elves were trying to pull her in to help Santa. Of course Obbie and I would go over and pull her out— and she would be so grateful!!

I remember Obbie and I would always try to find the largest socks we could find to hang up. In those days you had to hang one of your own socks. I think ours were usually knee socks that we hung. We always went to bed early that night—all excited.

Back then the decorations were always red and green. Not every color like they are today. My mother always made red and green Jell-O.

Our Christmas's were always very elaborate. We were told not to get up too early because we might scare Santa Claus away! We slept upstairs and my father used to come and slap the stairs during the night with his hands to make us think it was Santa. Another thing he would do was sneak outside and throw snowballs up on the roof so that we would think it was Santa! We (Obbie and I) were both *true believers*.

Invariably one of us would wake up between 12 and 1 o'clock and wake the other. We would sneak downstairs very quietly, so as not to scare Santa, and feel around to see if our stockings were full. When we found they were, we would put the light on. We always had lots of presents and our stockings were full of candy, nuts, a harmonica, and an orange. We were always so excited that we made a lot of noise, and my mother would come down and tell us it was too early, and that we had to go back to bed. But that was all right with us—now that we knew Santa had been there!!

I remember one year though, that she was so mad. I got a doll that year—one of the first that wet its pants. But we also got roller skates. In those days we didn't have carpeting in the dining rooms. We had large pieces of linoleum. Obbie and I put the skates on, and we were falling all over the place. I remember grabbing the table as I slipped underneath it on my rear end. We made such a racket that night that we each got a few whacks on the way up the stairs, because we were waking everyone up in the house!!

I can still remember that day outside the Osterville schoolhouse when Virginia Lewis told me that there wasn't any Santa. I can remember my heart just sinking! I was in the first or second grade - I can't remember which. All I can remember was how disappointed I was.

All of the other holidays were exciting in our house, too.

My folks didn't go to church, but I can remember the Baptist minister coming to our house every Wednesday evening for prayer meetings. They were especially excited one year when a new minister came to town and they knew him—a Reverend McDonald from Canada.

We were never allowed to play cards, or any other game, on Sunday. We were taught to keep the day Sabbath. No hard labor could be done, not even laundry. It was a day of rest.

When Obbie and I were about four or five years old, we started attending Sunday school which was before church at the Baptist Church each Sunday. I have some of the happiest memories of that church, and when I think back on it now. I will always have a soft spot for that church.

On Easter each year we always got up about 4 o'clock in the morning to attend the Easter Sunrise Service at Sunset Hill in Hyannisport near the Kennedy compound. Somebody always picked me up about 4:30 AM and it was dark outside. I always had a new coat, dress, shoes, hat and everything else new. Of course they were all light weight, because that was supposed to symbolize the beginning of Spring, in addition to the rising of the Lord. We almost froze to death standing around waiting for the service to end—and watching the sunrise!

However, afterwards, we were rewarded by some of the most delicious breakfasts I have ever had in my whole life. (At least, it seems that way now!) We had bacon, eggs, toast and hot chocolate. Then we had a brief church service, and then we went home.

Easter Bunny never forgot us either. On Easter morning when we would get up to go to the church service, our little parchment Easter Bunny container was always there beside the bed full of candy eggs.

Ronald and Grace Chesbro played a big part in the church then. We had a lot of fun times—with lots of parties. We put on several benefit plays where we sold tickets for the benefit of the church. I can't remember any of the names of the plays, but I can remember how much fun they were and how good they were.

And then there were the parties! Unlike today there wasn't any age limit. From the smallest—up through the teens—or so it seemed. Andrew Hall must be at least five years older than I. Then there was Carleton Hall, Dexter Patterson, Manning Hodges, Audrey and Virginia Allen, the Souzas (Betty and Doris) from the Plains, which is now called Marstons Mills, Dotty Coleman and all of the Whiteleys, Pat and Beverley, and Hope and Julia. I'm sure there were others whom I can't remember.

Back Row: Ronald Chesbro, Louis Williams, Andrew Hall, Virginia Allen, Manning Hodges,
Front: Pat Whiteley, Beverley Whiteley, Pearl, Audrey Allen, unknown, Dorothy Coleman.

We always bobbed for apples (and got our heads all wet) and played other games such as Post Office and Spin-the-Bottle! I can remember one time when we were playing Post Office. In that game there is always someone in a closet or room. Everybody has a number, the boys even and the girls uneven, or vice versa. The person in the room calls a number and that person has to go in and kiss the person in the room. And then that person can go out and the person left in there calls another number. I can remember calling Andrew Hall's number and then hiding beneath the old black stove which was in the room. I remember Andrew coming out and saying there wasn't anyone in there! Of course they came to look for me and they found me crouched way up against the wall underneath the old black stove!

We also had a lot of scavenger hunts in those days where we would walk all over town getting the necessary items.

In those days the population was so small that we all knew each other in town. We never locked our doors. And we never worried about kidnappers or thefts. Even the car keys were always left in the cars. (Nights, as well as when we went shopping.) We thought nothing of walking through the woods at night. The only thing we had to worry about was bumping into one of the town drunks once in a while. But usually they would fall over or not be able to walk!

Now to get back to my younger days again. There is so much I haven't told you!

On May Day each year, my mother would always hang us kids May baskets. She would decorate a cardboard shoe box or some other small box with crepe paper and fill it full of candy and cookies. It was always a SURPRISE. We would find it on the ground behind us - or just outside the door—any place that would be a surprise. We were always so happy!

Then another time I can remember my mother baking us a Gingerbread man with raisin buttons. She had it on the table. The next thing I knew, she was flying out the door screeching her head off, yelling that the Gingerbread man was running away! Of course Obbie and I took off after her almost all the way around the house before she caught it!

Mothers were homemakers in those days. My mother had a sewing machine and made many of my clothes when I was small. She also did a lot of baking. We always had desserts: apple, pumpkin, mince, lemon meringue or rhubarb pie, all kinds of cakes, and puddings. Chocolate nut pudding was my favorite. Also she often made bread. The house always smelled so good! After the bread had finished rising on the back of the stove, and before she put it in the oven to bake, she would cut off several pieces and fry them in the frying pan. They were so delicious I can almost taste it now.

My father always had chickens, so we always had plenty of eggs—and plenty of chicken to eat. I can almost remember the first time he chopped the head off a rooster and how upset I was. After seeing that poor bird flop around on the ground, I don't think I was too happy about eating chicken for a while. From then on I think I made myself scarce when I knew he was going out to retrieve a chicken for dinner!!

But my mother did make the most delicious chicken stew, with dough boys. We didn't call them dumplings then; they were dough boys.

Every once in a while we would get an ugly rooster. He would always manage to get out of the hen pen and have the complete freedom of our yard. If anyone went near him, he would jump up and bite them. On more than one occasion my mother would be attacked while out hanging clothes on the clothesline. She would come flying in the house cussing that ugly rooster! Then, when the rooster got old and it came time for my father to kill him, we would all cry and claim that we weren't going to eat any of the meat. But, of course, we did.

We also hatched our own baby chicks. My folks could always tell when we had a "setting" hen when they couldn't get her off the nest. To this day I still don't know how they could tell which eggs were fertilized and would turn into a baby chick! But just about every egg they put under that chicken produced a little one. They were so cute when they were born and it was such fun watching them crack the shells to come into the world. My father use to put some of them into a homemade incubator, made with light bulbs, to keep them warm.

We also had a pig one year. We got it in early spring, just a wee little one. But it grew very fast. We gave it lots of food and it became a member of our family!! We all loved it. The odor and flying insects didn't Seem to bother us. It was a member of our family!

In the fall, my father hired a man to come to the house to slaughter the pig. He didn't tell any of us kids about it. But the next thing we knew the pig was hanging in the woods. Why, we all cried and carried on and none of us were ever going to eat any of that meat!! (Even my mother cried.) But, of course, we did. I think even my father was upset. We never did have another Pig!

From the time I was little, my father always did have a car. I must tell you this, because, once again, we always ended up crying. He bought his first car in New Bedford. (When they first came over from New Brunswick, Canada, that was where they settled.) About every three years after

My dear father

that a Jewish man from New Bedford would come down with another used car to show my father. He must have been a good salesman, because it seems my father always ended up trading in the old one!! He would always come back within a day or

16

two to pick up the money and drive the old car away. Once again, we were all so sad saying good-bye to the old car. We all stood in the door and cried, even my mother! It's so funny, what should have been a happy event always turned out to be so sad!

I can remember when I was probably about four years old. I can even remember where I was standing - outside the porch on the lawn. My mother came out and said, "Don't go away, don't go too far from home, Polio is going around." well I thought polio was a truck or something that came around and took us away. So I sure stayed close to home that day, and I can't remember how many other days!! Sometime later on I learned that polio was a disease, but I can still remember how scared I was.

I think my personality make-up has always included being a bit gullible. (Even though I pride myself with having a lot of common sense.) When I was about nine, I had my tonsils and adenoids out. To make me feel good about my trip to the hospital my mother told me I could order anything I wanted while I was in there! So, of course, the first thing I thought about ordering was a bicycle!!

I never will forget that trip to the hospital, the ether mask being placed over my nose and the BONG, BONG, BONG in my head while counting backwards from ten before passing into oblivion. When I came to, I couldn't even swallow my own saliva, my throat was so sore! However I managed to recover a little bit each day. On the second day, I was able to get a little chicken with rice soup down. By the tenth day I was back swimming like a fish in the pond.

Left to right: Pearl, Ed, Obbie (in the back), Arthur, Polly, and Kenny.

Now I must mention the flowers in those days. They were so beautiful and they were all wild. We had patches of black-eyed susans, lily-of-the-valley, May flowers, violets and several lilac bushes. Plus orange tiger lilies, goldenrod, and another small blue flower which grew over the hill (I never did know the name), and honeysuckle, which always smelled so nice.

We always had lots of birds. I can remember waking up to the tune of "COO-COO-COO", which were the doves off in the distance. Another bird, which I don't think I have heard since I returned to the Cape to retire, is the "CHICK-A-DEE-DEE-DEE-DEE-DEE." They always answered each other all day long when we were little. It always sounded so cute.

At night we would go to sleep to the tune of the frogs croaking in the ponds and swamps. Some of them were so loud and coarse sounding. (We called them Grandfather Frogs.) Others made different croaks, but it sure sounded as though there were a lot of them down there.

The grass had lots of grasshoppers and we had many beautiful butterflies. Obbie and I use to follow them around and try to catch them.

I remember one night we took jars and caught a lot of lightning bugs. We put holes in the top of the jars so that the lightning bugs could breathe. I made mine too large. That night after going to bed and putting the light out, I was some surprised to see all of these lightning bugs flying all over the room! Of course I tried to catch them all again, but I'm sure I was not successful.

We always had cats. There always seemed to be a stray that would come to our house, and we would feed it and give it a home. Many kittens were born at our place. I didn't learn until years later that a lot of them went into Sam's Pond in a burlap bag! I remember peeking into a closet once after one of the cats had given birth and seeing the cat eating the after-birth—which turned my stomach. I guess cats do that, I don't know.

The two kittens I remember the most were Crisco and Spry. They were born at our place and they were so cute. When they were little, they would crawl up the curtains or up my mother's leg, leaving snags in her good silk stockings. She got upset, but she still thought they were cute.

Another incident I must tell you about is the snake I encountered on my way through the path to Joshua's Pond. It was a fairly large black snake. I didn't see the little ones at first, but when the snake saw me, it opened its mouth. Three little baby snakes, each about six inches long, slid into its mouth. And the snake slithered away. I never did forget that, it was so fascinating. I don't know whether anybody ever did believe me when I told them about that, but I really did see it.

In those days there wasn't any such thing as the flu or virus. We use to have attacks of bad stomach pains when we would throw up and not be able to keep anything down. It was called "the grippe". (I guess that is how you would spell it.) It would last two or three days. It was probably food poisoning, but we called it the grippe. Other than the grippe and childhood diseases and a cold now and then, we all stayed pretty healthy.

None of us were fat, but we were healthy. When I was in the first grade, I can remember my mother putting two pair of long stockings on me because my legs were so skinny. I can remember her giving me a teaspoon of Scotts Emulsion each day (I don't know what good that was supposed to do) and a teaspoon of Cod Liver Oil! I can remember I weighed 72lbs. when I was in the seventh grade.

Oh yes, before I forget this, the Whiteleys had a cow. They use to move it around from time to time to graze in the different fields. Every once in a while they would put it in the field right outside our kitchen window where we would have to watch it crap and stick its tongue up its nose while we were eating! That was another thing that my mother complained about. But I don't think she ever did say anything to the Whiteleys, and neither did us kids, because we were taught very young that you don't carry any tales out of the house. She said we should always remember that "It's a dirty bird that will shit in its own nest!" And I don't think any of us ever forgot that!

We always had our milk delivered in those days. Every morning when we got up, it would be on the front step. In the winter it would be frozen and the cream would be sticking way up out of the narrow-neck bottle.

A fish truck also came around once in a while. My mother would sometimes buy fish. If the driver had eels, she would always buy an eel or two. We all loved eels. That meat is so good! But have you ever watched an eel being fried in a frying pan? – It squirms all over even though it is cut up into two-inch pieces! (Eels were rolled in corn meal before frying.)

I should interject here that even though we were a healthy family, we were not immune to some bizarre happenings.

On the fourth of July each year we always had fireworks. They were not illegal then. We always had firecrackers, sparklers, rockets and snakes (little buttons that, when set on fire, would pop up and curl around like a snake). One year we were standing on the porch lighting firecrackers and throwing them out in the yard. One of the firecrackers did not go off. Ed went out and picked it up and puffed on it, like a cigarette. Well, it went off all right—right in Ed's mouth. (Ed was about five years old at the time.)

My poor mother came running out and even though she did not know how to drive, she drove him down to Dr. Kinny's office. (My father was laid up at the time with a broken back. He had fallen out of one of the apple trees in our yard with one of those large spray cans on his back.) Fortunately for Ed, all he had was a bunch of bad cuts in his mouth and throat. My mother thought he had blown his palate off.

Another time when we were all out in the yard and my mother was hanging clothes, we heard all this screeching coming from inside the house. We all went running in and there was little Arthur with his arm completely through the washing machine wringer. The wringer was still going around, taking the skin off his underarm. It's a wonder it didn't pull the arm out of the socket, but I guess my mother got in there in time. (I don't remember how old Arthur was then, probably about two or three.)

And now for one other incident with Arthur when he was about the same age. The Cushman Truck always came around in those days selling bread and goodies. One day after my mother had made a purchase, she turned around just in time to see the truck pulling away with Arthur hanging on the back. He was holding onto the bumper with both hands while being dragged down the street.

Well, my mother took off screeching at the top of her lungs to try to stop the Cushman truck. Fortunately for her, Agnes Sears was out in the yard hanging clothes on the clothesline on Pond Street. She heard my mother screeching and stopped the Cushman truck. Arthur was lucky because the road from our house to Pond Street was a dirt road. If he had been dragged any distance on Pond Street, he would have received a lot more than skin off both knees. But the biggest miracle of all here was that the truck did not back up and run over him!

Obbie, Polly, Pearl and little Arthur

Another time Obbie, Ed, Arthur and I all went over to Sonny Moran's on Pond Street to see his pig that had had some baby pigs. We no sooner got over there than little Arthur said he was going home. So he turned around and started home. The rest of us all watched the baby pigs for a while and then we decided to go home. As we were walking into our yard, my mother came out and said, "Where is Arthur?" We said, "He came home." She said, "No, he didn't!" Well, we looked all over, and nobody could find little Arthur anywhere. Mrs. Whiteley came out, and all of the Whiteley kids, and we all shouted and called and went down around both ponds looking for little Arthur. My mother and Mrs. Whiteley both completely ruined their silk stockings walking through briars and thickets around the ponds. But still no Arthur. Finally, after about an hour of frantic searching, I can remember I was out on Bumps River Road (an extension of Pond Street) still shouting my lungs out, when a police cruiser came along with little Arthur in the front seat. It seems a slow-moving tractor had come along and had seen little Arthur walking on the street by himself. The driver probably figured he was too small to be by himself, so he picked him up and took him all the way over to Hyannis to the Police Station.

There were other little less earth-shattering instances that happened during my childhood, too, such as fish hook incidents. Every once in a while one of us would get a fish hook stuck in us which sometimes required the help of the Doctor to remove. I guess you might say that our lives were never dull in those days !

Now I must tell you a little about Agnes (Agnes Sears). She was one of my mother's few friends in town, who visited her often. (My mother was a homebody. In our younger years she never left the house except for our Saturday night jaunt to Hyannis.) Now Agnes was one of those vivacious, colorful people with personality PLUS. I can remember one time when she came to visit us when my father was home. She started off by saying, "God damn it, Martha, and Shit, Fraser," and then she went on to tell them whatever she had to say!! Even us kids always loved to see her come. She and Mrs. Whiteley. They were the "highlights" of our days on many occasions. Bear in mind, there were no TV's in those days.

And I should tell you here that we were also probably one of the last in town to have a phone put in. I think I was about twelve years old. They were all party lines then. Four homes were tied into one line.

I shouldn't tell you this but my mother and I enjoyed listening in to many of the conversations. We wouldn't deliberately check the line to see if anyone was on there, but if we picked it up to use and there was somebody talking, it was a great temptation not to listen in!!

But I also should tell you that when somebody was trying to reach one of the four parties on our line, the phone would ring in all four houses. One ring for the Whiteleys, two short rings for our house, etc.! So sometimes we would very quietly pick it up also, just to see who was talking!!

When we got a little older, we (Obbie, Pat, Beverley, and I) started building forts and underground tunnels. We would spend hours, and sometimes days, digging and building. We would cover the forts with old blankets, top and sides, and then sleep out in them at night.

I remember one of the houses we built was out by our hen house. We made it from some of my father's old pieces of wood. It had a door with a lock on it. It was about six feet by six feet and we built a bunk bed on each side inside. It was rather crude, but it had tar paper on the roof. That night Beverley and I were sleeping out. We had the door locked and felt very safe. That night in the middle of the night there was a torrential downpour with one of the most violent thunder and lightning storms I have ever lived through. The thunder sounded as though it was hitting between our fort and the hen pen in VERY loud bangs. Needless to say, Beverley and I were very scared. We hopped out of bed, grabbed the lantern, and ran through my father's garden to the house. My mother had gotten out of bed and was watching us come through the garden from the pantry. We learned later that night that a ball of lightning had entered the bedroom where Pat (Beverley's sister) was sleeping during the storm. If Beverley had been at home that night, she would have been in the same room; so, who knows, sleeping out may have saved her life that night!!

The tunnels that we would dig underground we would cover with pieces of wood, leaving an entryway so that we could get in. Then we would cover the wood all over with pine needles. We called them "pine-diddle-de-dees" in those days.

Which reminds me, when the fall came each year, we kids would always have to take the wheel barrow and gather up all the "pine-diddle-de-dees" in the woods in back of our house and place them up against the foundation of our house to keep it warm in the winter!!

In time a nice little old man moved into our neighborhood. His name was Ole Krosvik. He was a Norwegian sailor. He built a one-room bungalow on the edge of the woods on the other side of Whiteleys. He probably was about 45 or 50 years old—a harmless, lonesome, kind old man. He was awful good to us kids. We probably hounded him to death when we were little. Every spring we would clean his house for him. He would pay us $2.00 and he was always giving us things. One year he gave us an old fashioned Victrola with a big horn on top. Another time he gave us a wine bottle with a ship inside. I would give anything to have some of those items now. They would be worth a lot of money.

One year he gave Obbie and me a small row boat, about four feet long. We used it to paddle across some of the deep gullies in the field by our house when they would fill up with rain water. We really did get some torrential downpours in those days.

Ole was also the one to treat each one of us kids to our first plane ride. I remember how fascinated I was to look down at

Pearl at age 12

the ponds. They appeared to be different colors. But as I said before, they were not polluted. Today they are probably all one big black blob.

As we grew older, we stopped going over to Ole's and our younger siblings took over.

Every once in a while in those days people would come to our house soliciting. Why they would ever trek up that old dirt road to solicit is beyond me, but they did. One day a gypsy came to the house. (That's what my mother said she was. She had on very colorful clothing.) She wanted to tell my mother's fortune from tea leaves. My mother said, "No", she wasn't interested. But before the gypsy left she said to my mother, "Well, I can tell you right now, you have a sister who is a nurse, and I can see nails all around your face." Well, that sort of shocked my mother, because she did have a sister who was a nurse, and my father was a carpenter.

Later that same day my mother said she was still thinking about it when she happened to notice a picture of my Aunt Dot on the piano in her nurse's uniform and cap! (It would have been visible from the door.) Then she looked outside and saw the garage door wide open displaying all of my father's sawhorses, lumber, and carpentry tools!! My mother and I got such a big bang out of that!

When I was ten or eleven, I started to baby-sit. I baby-sat for Agnes and Pop Sears all the time. I can remember they had me two nights in a row one time. They were out very late both nights. The second night when they came home, I was sound asleep on the couch. They couldn't arouse me any way. They finally had to crawl in through a window! Then they woke me up and paid me 50 cents and I ran home. (They lived in the house that we moved from on Pond Street.)

One night when I had run home from their place about midnight, I ran up on our porch and was squirted by a skunk. What an odor! My mother came running downstairs and I think she put all of my clothes outside. I never was able to wear the coat again.

I often think back on my baby-sitting days, and I know that today, if I had a daughter, I would NEVER let her baby-sit. When I was about thirteen, I baby-sat for a Lieutenant Ogden, who lived up near the center of town. I baby-sat for them many times and I never had a problem. They had a daughter about one and a half years old. Then they moved to Marstons Mills. The Mrs. was expecting again. She called for me to baby-sit and asked if I would stay overnight and go to the beach with them the next day so that I could watch the little one. I wasn't too enthused about that, but I said "yes" anyway.

That night about 5 o'clock the Lieutenant came to pick me up. He asked if I would mind going with him over to Hyannis to pick up his dry cleaning. I said O.K. But instead he drove over to Yarmouth to the Mill Hill Club where I sat outside in the car for half an hour. Then he came out, and I thought he was taking me to his house. We went through Osterville towards Marstons Mills. Finally we came to an old dirt road, which he turned down. It was so narrow that the overgrown growth was scratching the outside of the car.

Finally he stopped, looked at me and said, "How about a kiss?" I was so scared, but I kept my senses. I lifted my left hand, let my fingers hang down and beckoned for him to move on. At the same time I was saying, "Get Going!" in a very authoritative voice. With that he started the car and we moved on, eventually arriving at his house. I was so scared that night. I didn't call my mother because I didn't know where I was. I wouldn't have been able to tell them how to get there. Needless to say, I put in one horrible night. The next day I went to the beach with them, but I couldn't wait for the day to end so I could get home. I never did tell my mother, but needless to say, I never did go back again either. (I often think back, if I had panicked or started to scream or something, he might have killed me! I think that is how some murders happen.)

My cute little brother, Kenny, who drank himself to death at age 36.

When I was thirteen, I had another very unpleasant experience. A family on Swift Avenue approached my mother and father to see if I could spend the summer with them. They had a boy and a girl about four and six that they wanted me to care for. I was to sleep at the house (because they went out a lot at night), with one day off a week (Monday), for $2.00 a week. They said we would go to Craigville Beach often where they had a Beach Locker. I don't remember ever agreeing to go, but I went. It was the longest summer I ever put in. I felt so alone. I had no one else to play with or talk to and no spare time of my own. I couldn't wait for the summer to get over. I would never wish a position like that on any girl.

Now that I have told you about a couple unpleasant experiences in my life, I must say they did not seem to harm me in any way. Except possibly to appreciate the privileges of FREEDOM all the more. Now keep that word in mind until you finish this book.

Now I will tell you a little bit about my father He was a good man, a hard worker. He worked for Daniel Brothers as a carpenter most of his life. He went to work every morning at7:30, returning at approximately 4:30 every afternoon. We always had dinner about five. Then he would sit in the chair or lay on the couch until Gabriel Heater came on the radio at six o'clock. None of us kids could talk when Gabriel Heater was on, because my father was hard of hearing. His ears were damaged while fighting in France during World War I.

Pearl at age fifteen with her father

He put in apple trees, and always had a garden with all kinds of vegetables: potatoes, carrots, beets, corn, beans, and peas. Also tomatoes, radishes, and strawberries. Obbie and I had the chore now and then of picking the bugs off the potato plants and putting them into a can with a little kerosene in it.

Every Spring Charlie Coleman would come with his horse and plow the garden. Then my father would take us kids, when the herring were running, to Marstons Mills. We each had a net. We would come back with several burlap bags of herring which he used for fertilizer in the garden. That was always lots of fun for Obbie and I. We would just about always fall in and come back with our feet all wet. In later years, when my father was gone, my younger brother, Kenny, use to catch them just for roe (eggs carried by the females). That was quite a delicacy, dipped in corn meal and fried.

My Childhood Years

My father was not one to pay a lot of attention to us kids. He was good to us. He would play baseball with us once in a while or take us to Hyannis with him, or something like that. But my mother was the organizer in our house, and she was also the disciplinarian. They went to Hyannis every Saturday night to do their grocery and other shopping. They usually took us kids with them. On the way back, when we would go by Dutchland Farms; we kids would always yell, "I scream, you scream, we all scream for ice cream!" Sometimes he would stop for ice cream cones, and sometimes he would not. I can remember the car was always so quiet when he didn't stop.

During the week my mother would send us kids up to Parker's Store when she needed something from the grocery store. They would let the town folks charge there. They kept a little tab in back and would add on when we bought something and subtract when we sent money. I can remember one time when my mother gave me a five dollar bill and sent me to the store. I went down Pond Street and up Main Street on roller skates. When I got there the five dollars was gone. I never did tell my mother I lost the money. To this day I still feel guilty when I think about it. That was a lot of money in those days. A few days later, I heard in school that Virginia Lewis had found a five dollar bill. I still never said a word.

During the winter we played a lot of games at our house. I can't remember us doing much homework; but we were always playing cards, Chinese checkers, or dominoes. Plus it seems there was always a puzzle on one of the tables for us to work on. During the fall and spring, especially in the late afternoon and evening, we played outside a lot. I guess you might say that our favorite games, in addition to baseball, were "Kick the Can" and "Hide and Seek".

My father was always in bed by 8:30. In the winter he always got up early and put coal in the stove and got the house warm, and then he would take the broom and tap on the ceiling for my mother to get up and get his breakfast and make his lunch.

My mother often made fudge at night. It was so good. She would drop a little bit into cold water when she was cooking it to see if it hardened; if it did, it was done. We would all take turns getting that tasty little bit from the spoon. Otherwise we would have to wait until she poured it into a pan and wait for it to harden. (We used several spoons to clean the pan.)

Sometimes in the evening, if we were hungry, we would cut up a raw potato, put it in a bowl, put vinegar over it and eat it with salt and pepper. Delicious!

The vegetables which we got out of the garden every summer (potatoes, carrots, onions) were always stored down cellar under the kitchen portion of our house, which was not finished off. The earth made it very cool down there, but not freezing. The vegetables usually lasted us most of the winter.

Picture of our house taken sometime before we bought it

Picture of our house taken in 1956

My father not only had a garden and apple trees. He also built a garage and remodeled the house. The kitchen was completely remodeled with a pantry added and the upstairs finished off with dormers added. When we moved in, there was a ladder in the dining room leading to a hole in the ceiling to get into the upstairs. He also added a porch. - Not to mention the hen house and the garage which he also built. Oh yes, and the foundation which he put in under the house, I must not forget to tell you about that. That was a big job. When we moved in there was a rock cellar under the house which was about eight feet by eight feet. The only thing down there was the fuse box. (Every once in a while the lights would all go out in the house. If my father did not have a fuse he would stick a penny in behind the old blown fuse and the lights would come on again!) Well, my father dug all of the dirt out from under the house all by himself. Wheelbarrow full by wheelbarrow full and dumped it at the top of the hill leading to Sam's Pond. As the hole got bigger and bigger under the house, he brought home jacks to hold the house up. And finally he was able to lay the cinder blocks.

The part under the kitchen was made larger but it was not finished off. Cinder blocks were not put in. A doorway opening was made but he deliberately did not do more so that we could continue to store our vegetables there.

Later he built a three-room bungalow on the back of our property which they rented out. It had a kitchen, living room, bedroom, and bathroom. Obbie later lived there when he got married, and then Arthur. Arthur eventually bought it. He has added a lovely family room, two more bedrooms and another bath. He fell heir to the garage and some additional property when my mother died. It is a beautiful piece of property now. The big house was sold.

I guess it's no wonder my poor father never had much time to spend with us kids, now that I think about it.

But I must tell you this one story that my father told us kids when we were little. I heard him tell this story to others on many occasions. There was a man who lived near him on the edge of a lake. He was a woodsman. One day he set out in his boat to go hunting on the other side of the lake. He told his dog to stay behind. (The dog usually did mind.) But every time he started out this time the dog followed, swimming after his boat. Finally he said, "I'll fix that dog!" So he took him home and tied him up with very strong rope. Then he started out again to cross the lake. When he got halfway across he turned around and he just couldn't believe it, but there was the darn dog again swimming after him. By now the man was really mad, so he turned around and took the dog home and CHOPPED HIS HEAD OFF!! "There now," he said. "That should take care of that dog!" Then he went back and started across the lake again. When he got almost to the other side he turned around and you will never believe what he saw! There came the dog, swimming across the lake—with its head in its mouth!!!

My father was always very frugal. He frowned on credit. We were taught when you made money to always save a little bit! We were also taught very young that you should not buy anything unless you have the cash to pay for it. We were one of the last in the town, I think, to have a refrigerator, because we had to pay CASH for ours.

The refrigerator. That was another story in itself!! I can remember when we got our first refrigerator. If we wanted anything out of it, we had to open the door and close it as fast as we could; otherwise it would be letting the cold air out and causing the motor to run. Now when I think back, I have to laugh! That night, every time the motor went on, we all looked at each other. My mother looked so worried. We were all sure we were going to receive a humongous electric bill!! After a few days though the novelty wore off and we didn't give it a thought any longer.

My father was not a drinker. He kept a bottle of whiskey on the top shelf in the pantry for medicinal purposes. If he was getting a cold, or thought he was getting sick, he would come home from work and take a swig right out of the bottle. (But that didn't happen very often.)

The couple of times I did see my mother and father have a drink was always on Halloween, which was my father's birthday. George and Celia Tibbits would always come over and they would play cards. They were good friends of my mother and father. But I must continue and tell you about Halloween. I have so many memories of that day that I don't know where to start. During the years when Polly was a teenager, all of the boys use to come to our house on that night. They would let the hens out of the hen house, turn all of the outdoor furniture upside down and soap the windows. And I don't know what else! My father and George would always go out and chase them away. One year they both took off out the door. My father went one way and George the other around the house. It was so dark in those days. They didn't see each other and ran smack into each other. George was a very robust man, and my father cracked his back and had to go to the doctor.

Another time I can remember my father going upstairs with a bucket of water and dumping it out the window completely soaking poor Chalmers Milne. He had to go home to change his clothes.

They always ended up catching some of the boys and bringing them in the house. Then the rest of the boys would come in and they all had popcorn, doughnuts, and apple cider. (I think the boys sometimes brought some of the food.) It was always the next morning before we discovered the damage!

Now for Obbie and I out trick or treating!! Early in the evening we would go out and string toilet paper across the street and hide in the woods. That was always fun seeing the cars slam to a stop.

We would go over to Rose Crocker's house on Pond Street and stick a pin into her doorbell. It would ring continuously until she came out and removed it. After we thought we had got her goat, we would go back and ring for trick or treat. One year after we did that, she came out and shoved us down the steps! We didn't go back for our treat. I don't think she would have given us any!!

Polly and Pearl

Another year we went down Fire Station Road where Jesse Murray kept the school bus, the one that took us to Junior High School each day. We took four spikes and put one behind each wheel so that when he backed up he would get four flat tires. Then we soaped the windows on both the inside and outside. We figured it would take them a long time to clear that off!! Well, guess what happened!!! The bus was on time. The front and back windows were cleared, but they didn't clean the side windows. We were unable to see anything out the side windows all the way to the school. So we were unable to see any of the other damage that was done that night. We were so disappointed. There was always a lot of damage done on Halloween. The older boys would put garbage cans up flag poles, smash pumpkins on the street, take property from some people's homes and put it on others, etc.

Another thing Obbie and I did when we were little. We had two tall fir trees in our front yard. (I was always a tomboy when I was young.) Whenever the fire whistle would blow, we would each take a tree and climb to the very top to see where the smoke was coming from. That would give us an idea where the fire was. Those trees had several crooked branches. Near the top on both trees there were straight branches and then crooked branches just above that, that sort of caught our backs. We called them "chairs"!

During the summer we had very hot spells. There wasn't a breath of air upstairs where we all slept. Nobody had air conditioning then. (Well, maybe the rich people did, but none of the townfolks.) I remember Obbie and I would take our pillows and blankets and go out and sleep on the lawn. We would put the blanket on the ground to sleep on.

Sometimes I slept on Whiteley's porch with Pat and Beverley. I can remember one time a bat got in on the porch and Mr. Whiteley had to come out and kill it. The Whiteleys also had a small cellar. Mr. Whiteley in those years made his own wine, which he kept down there in a big barrel with a spigot. One day the four of us, Pat, Beverley, Obbie and I, each poured ourselves a glassful of the wine. We were going to see who could drink the whole glass. Pat, Beverley, and I didn't like it, so we didn't drink much. But Obbie, trying to show us what a man he was, drank the whole glassful. On the way home he kept falling down. (He was drunk!) My mother, seeing him stumble through the fence between our properties, knew something was wrong. She came out and took him in the house. She called the Doctor and he told her to let him sleep it off, which she did! I don't remember anything happening to me, but I know Pat and Beverley got spanked. Obbie must have been only about five years old at the time.

My Teenage Years

Now I'll tell you a little bit about my school days. I can't say that I was ever one of the best students there ever was. In the subjects I was interested in, I did very well (Math, English, Civics, and Business Courses). In the subjects I didn't like, I bluffed and cheated my way all through school. (Those subjects were History, Geography, and Myths.) I can remember when I was in the seventh grade. I had Ma Hurst for Myths. Julia Whiteley sat in front of me. She was smart. She would lean to one side when we had exams so that I could see her answers. (Of course, I would change a few so that the teacher wouldn't be suspicious.) Oh, how I hated that class.

In History I can remember writing names and dates in ink all over the inside of my hands and nails. The teacher was always giving quizzes. After I would write the answer down, I would lick it off with my tongue. I usually barely made it through those subjects.

Now that I think back on my High School days, I was really quite active. I always had a lot of friends and there wasn't much I didn't do! I always managed to find someone to pick me up to go to all of the basketball and football games.

Priscilla Wittenmeyer was one of my closest friends. She had a car all through High School. It was a used car and wasn't in very good condition, but it always managed to get us where we wanted to go. I remember one time when five of us girls decided to go up to Boston in Priscilla's car to the Old Howard, a striptease joint. None of us were eighteen years old. I remember how scared I was every time the Police walked up and down the aisle. I kept expecting them to ask how old we were. A bunch of Canadian sailors sat right behind us. All I can remember now about the show was a man coming out on stage with a long pole with a swab on the end of it. He said he was giving Superman a douche?! We stayed at the Hotel that night near South Station. I can remember we all had Tom Collins delivered to the room by room service. I guess we were all sowing our wild oats that night! But we had a good time.

Another time I can remember when we went up to Boston to a basketball tournament in Priscilla's car. Every time we had to stop at a red light, the car would stall. We would all jump out and get someone behind us to push us. Bobby Lorrange from Cotuit was the only fellow in our car. One time we got a push from the Wonder Bread Truck. When he pushed us, his truck bumper slid up over the two prongs on our rear bumper and stuck. Of course we all jumped up and down on our bumper trying to get the Wonder Bread front bumper to slip up over and off our bumper. We finally got one side up over, but it came down on one girl's foot. She started screeching and crying. Bobby Lorrange managed to get the jack out of the car and was able to lift it just enough to get her foot out. He also managed, in time, to get the Wonder Bread off our bumper. Of course, we thanked the Wonder Bread man and told him we would eat only Wonder Bread from now on!! Then we got someone else to give us a push!

Now, when I think back on those days, I don't know how I managed to do so much. I took part in sports. I was on the basketball team and the field hockey team, and I worked. When I became sixteen, I got a job after school at the Osterville News Stand working for Margaret Hansberry. There was a very popular Soda Fountain there and in addition to my other duties, I was put in charge of the supplies, which included mixing all of the sugar water. On Sundays I had to be at work at 6 AM to put the Sunday newspapers together with the other girls. The store always opened early on Sunday because there were always some early risers who wanted their papers early. It was always a mad house right after Church.

In addition to working, sports, school, and baby-sitting, I also dated. I had my first date on New Year's Eve when I was thirteen. His name was Sparkie Bowman, and I met him at a Youth Fellowship Meeting in Falmouth. I can't remember what we did but I think we just rode around that night stopping to get something to eat. I know I was home early, about ten o'clock.

When I was a teenager, I changed from the Baptist Church to the Community Church (Methodist) all because many of my friends were in the Youth Fellowship in that church. I had some great times in that church, too, but when I think back now, I don't know how I could have abandoned that good Baptist Church where I had so many great times. They were so good to me.

The summer after I turned sixteen, I went to work at East Bay Lodge as a waitress. I had a room there and stayed there nights. We called them dormitories. We had to get up at six every morning because we had to have the tables ready and be on our toes when the people started coming in at seven. That was a job I wasn't very happy with either. I don't think I was ever happy when I had to sleep away from home. I know I didn't sleep well, and I had to do my own laundry, which I wasn't used to either.

One night one of the girls who worked there, Shirley Tolen from Braintree, talked me into going over to Yarmouth when we got off work to go to the Carnival. We went by taxi. We weren't there very long before two fellows started hanging around us. They were in the Navy. We spent most of the evening walking around and going on rides with them. I don't remember who paid. I think we all paid our own. But, at any rate, they had a car and ended up giving us a ride home. Shirley must have liked the one she picked, because I was in the front seat, and every time I turned around, they were going to town kissing. When we arrived at East Bay, I don't remember where they went; the fellow that I was with and I went for a walk down East Bay Road. He was very polite and mannerly. I never did see him again. Never did I ever go out with Shirley again, either.

After that summer I never did go back to East Bay Lodge to work because that Fall was when I got the job at the Osterville News Stand. So I worked there the rest of my High School days (Summers full time and Winters after school). Margaret was very good to work for and I loved working there. The girls I worked with were a lot of fun (Mildred Linnell, Virginia Lewis and Elinor Stever). Thinking back on it now, those were probably the happiest years of my life. Those were the years when my time was fully occupied. School, sports and games, working a lot, and socializing and dating in what time was left. When I wasn't dating I had the money to pay my own way, so that made it VERY pleasant.

In those days, a date was a trip to the movies or bowling. - Always getting a coke, or French fries (or both) afterwards. The movie house could be anywhere from Buzzard's Bay to Orleans. And so could the bowling alleys. I was never promiscuous. Neither were the boys in those days. The big thing then was to get a good-night kiss. We didn't know about sex in those days. At least I didn't.

I should tell you here that Polly was the one who paved the way for my teenage years. As I told you before, she was different from me. She was "close-faced"! She never told my mother where she was going or whom she was going with. Consequently, my mother was always waiting up for her when she went out. I can remember one night when she went out with Jimmy or Danny Flynn, I don't remember which. When she came home she had liquor on her breath, and I can remember my mother whacking her all the way up the stairs!

When it came time for me to go out, I was always "open-faced". I always told my mother where I was going and whom I was going with. Later I would tell her some of the things that happened. Consequently, I guess my mother felt at ease with me and never gave me a problem.

Me at seventeen

After I graduated from High School, I went home one night and Miss Margerie Leonard was there. She said she needed someone to work in her insurance office, which was a few doors down from the News Stand. She said she had been over to the school and Miss Hayden had recommended me! I was getting $16.00 a week at the News Stand, so she would pay me $18.00. I can remember how disappointed I was. But it was more money and an opportunity to get ahead, according to my parents. Once again, I don't remember accepting, but I went. I can't say it was a bad job. I enjoyed the work and Miss Leonard was very good to work for, but it just wasn't the same as the freedom and the people I enjoyed at the News Stand! I stayed with Miss Leonard for five years until I married and had my first child.

Now, back to my High School Days again. When I was in about the 11th grade, someone told me that Janet Murray's cousin was moving to Osterville. (Little did I realize that he would be the one I would end up spending most of my life with!) When he arrived in Osterville, he went to work right away for his uncle, Jesse Murray, on the ice truck. That's when I saw him for the first time! When he drove in the yard to deliver ice to our house (with Janet beside him), I saw him coming and ran up the stairs and peeked around the curtains to see what he looked like. (I can't remember thinking anything either one way or the other.)

My mother always said he was the worst ice man she had ever had! He would put the ice right on the kitchen floor to crack it to get a piece that would fit in the ice box. Then my mother would grumble and groan cleaning it up after he left. All of the other ice men had taken the ice outside to crack it.

During the summer I was down swimming in the pond late one afternoon. (Probably after work). I was the only one there when a car pulled up. It was Janet's cousin. As he was coming down the bank to the pond, I decided to come out of the water and go home. We passed each other at just about the water's edge, not speaking. He always said he thought I was Betsy Verkade that day, because she also had a red bathing suit!

He always sat in the front of the bus with his friends. And I always sat with my friends in the back. I don't think we ever did speak. I can remember noticing him though. I couldn't help noticing his neck. I remember thinking that fellow had the biggest and widest neck I had ever seen!

He turned out to be one of the star performers on our football team, and I can remember watching him perform many of his miracles at many of our games. (That still didn't mean anything to me though. I was rooting for the whole team!)

My Favorite picture of Howard

Then one day in my senior year (I was one year ahead of Howard and ten months older), he came into the News Stand to ask me to go to the Junior Prom with him. I told him, "No, I already have a date that night with a Marine," which I did not. (He has often told me since then, how embarrassed he was, being turned down in front of all those people. He now says he doesn't know how he had the courage!)

Several months later my Senior Banquet came up—and I needed an escort. I couldn't have been going with anyone special at the time, so my thoughts were that I would ask Howard. Since I had already turned him down, I wouldn't feel so bad if he turned me down! I cornered him on the way down the hill by old Dr. Kinney's. But when I asked him if he would like to go with me he said, "Yes."

A few days before the Banquet, he came to the house one day. I opened the door about six inches to see what he wanted. He asked what I would like for a corsage; what color. I told him a pink carnation would be fine, and he left. Well, my Aunt Dot was visiting from New York at the time and she flew into a rage. She said, "Now, Pearl, that was very rude. I am going to have to take you to New York and give you a Coming Out Party and teach you some manners. You should have invited that fellow into the house, introduced him to all of us, and told him you wanted an ORCHID!!" I never will forget that. I really thought she was serious, but I never did go to New York.

Well, Janet's cousin Howard and I went to the Banquet with Cynthia Lewis and Buddy McLane, and we had a good time. After that I saw Howard once in a while. He would give me rides home from the softball games quite often. Plus, that summer we were always in the same crowd at the beach. I can't quite remember how many times we went out that year, but I do know that by the end of his senior year, he was asking me out a lot. He would come over to the house often, too. Sometimes he would come over and peek in the window and say he was hungry. (That was his way of getting inside!) I would always make him a tomato and lettuce sandwich or something.

HS Senior Prom 1946

That was about when the chemistry kicked in. I liked him and I knew he liked me. I can remember one time when we went to the movies. He reached over and took my hand. It sent shock waves up my back. I never had that happen with any of my other boyfriends. (Nor has it happened since.)

That summer after he graduated was such a fun summer for me. I was in love. We not only dated singly, but we double-dated a lot, too. I can remember one date when we went out with Arthur Williams and Agnes Shields. They took us down to the Orleans Inn where the platform was out over the water. The boys didn't have much money then, but right after the hostess seated us they ordered four rye and ginger drinks, and then excused themselves to go to the restroom. Well, while they were gone, the waitress came with the drinks. I took one look at Agnes and said "What do you say we drink these all up and tell the boys the waitress brought four empty glasses!" So Agnes drank Art's and I downed Howard's and mine. When the fellows came back we took one look at them and started to laugh. I can still remember the looks on their faces when they admitted they didn't have any more money; which made it all the funnier to Agnes and I. So we had to leave. Well, Agnes and I couldn't stop laughing. And it was all we could do to walk out the door.

I had many fun dates that year. When we weren't going to the movies or bowling, we would ride up to the Bourne Bridge where we would order a container of fried clams. They were so good, but I would always have to send Howard in for more salt. We would eat them in the car. Those were the fun days with no cares.

Our weekends were spent on the beach, or in the sailboat. Howard had a sailboat which we went out in often. I can remember more than one bad sunburn from spending the day out on one of those islands.

Now I think it was during this time frame on one of these hot summer nights during the wee hours of the morning that I was awakened by a tremendous crash. I learned the next day that it was Charlie Kalas arriving home from a night out on the town. He missed the curve and tried to drive over the raised island memorial for World War I veterans in front of the Country Store, which was where he lived. Pieces of his car could still be seen here and there several days later. I know he got hurt, but I don't remember how badly.

Finally the summer ended, September was here, and Howard, who had signed up for two years in the Army, had to leave. I will always remember that last date. We stayed out until four in the morning. Just kissing. He didn't want to leave—and I didn't want to see him go! The next day he left for the Army. He was sent to Ft. Knox, Kentucky, for his boot training. He was gone eight weeks before returning on a couple weeks furlough. We relished that short time together, and then he was off to Korea.

Howard at Boot Camp

After he left for Korea, I may have received a few letters from him, but then they ceased. I didn't hear from him, and all of the mail I sent was returned "unknown". What I didn't know was that he became ill on the ship on the way over to Korea and was sent to a hospital with scarlet fever for a couple of weeks. When he was released, he was put in with a different group. And the mail wasn't able to keep up with him.

I remember the package I had sent him for Christmas. It included a pen and pencil set, writing paper (to write to me), a wallet, chocolate bars, and I can't remember what else. I filled in all the crevices with mixed nuts. In January, the package came back to me, unopened, with a hole in one corner, and the nuts rolling all over the Osterville Post Office.

After that disappointing episode, I started to receive letters again. But by that time I had also started to date again. A new fellow, working behind the soda fountain at the Osterville Drug Store, asked me out. His name was Martin Anderson. It turned out, or so he confided in me, that he was a detective, brought into the store because someone had been pilfering money. He was trying to keep track of any money wrung up in the registers. I went with him for several months. I can't remember anything that exciting that we did. I think I was more fascinated by the fact he was a detective. I visited his home in Belmont one weekend. His father was an importer, and Martin showed me his name listed in the book of Who's Who in America, or United States, or whatever. They had a lovely big home. My father always referred to Martin as the Aristocrat! After he left the Drug Store, he came down to visit me one weekend in his father's big Cadillac. Another weekend I visited him at Dartmouth College where he had invited me to some kind of Campus weekend. I really didn't have that great a time because I felt out of place and didn't know anyone other than Martin.

It was during the time I was going with him at the Drug Store that I sent the "Dear John" letter to poor Howard telling him that I had a new boyfriend. Shortly after that I received a very nice package from Howard - a Korean kimono. I wrote and thanked him and I think I sent a few more letters, but by then his letters had cooled and I stopped writing altogether.

When the two years were up, another girl, who was interested in Howard, stopped me uptown one day and told me Howard was coming home. She asked me if he asked me out if I would go. (I know she was hoping I would say "no".) I said, "Sure, why not?"

Two days later someone told me he was home. That night I called his house to tell him "Welcome Home." He wasn't home so I told his mother I had called to welcome him home. The next day, when I was on my way to lunch at the Drug Store, who should pull up, and go in to have lunch with me but Howard. It was just like old times. I was so excited I never did finish my hamburger!

He asked me out that night. Of course, I said "Yes" even though I had another date that night with Buzzy McKinny from Yarmouth. I rushed into the pay phone after work at the News Stand and left a message with Buzzy's father that I would not be able to go out that night because we had company from Canada!!

On the way home that night who should come along to give me a ride home but Howard. He was driving very slow, but he came so close he actually hit the back of my knees. That was the beginning of our two-year torrid love affair before we became engaged.

Now let me tell you a little bit about Howard. Howard is a good man, a kind man, an honest man. However, he does have one flaw. I call it the "Riedel quirk." His mother had the same type personality. They say things that do not always come out right. But I shouldn't say that either, because sometimes they do come out right! (In their "humorous" sarcasm, they are sometimes really being serious.)

That was my one problem all during my married life with Howard. When I was young, I was a very sensitive person. In fact, I still am. Howard could only stay nice so long. Maybe a week, two weeks, or a month. But sooner or later the little sarcastic digs would come out, and I would give

David Crosby's Car

him the silent treatment for a day— or two OR THREE. It was a good thing I didn't have any place to go, otherwise I would have been long gone. However the sun would always come out. And before long everything was back to normal again.

Now that we are older, or what I should say, is that over the years, I became a little more outspoken, and now I speak up when he says something I don't like. (Every once in a while now he tells me that everything has broken down on me, except my MOUTH.)

Now back to our courting days. One time we went to Peter's Pond House in Forestdale with several of our friends for "Happy Hour." While we were there it started to snow all the harder and everything was turning to ice, so we decided we had better head home. Howard and I rode in David Crosby's car. Frankie Boyne and a car load of other kids were right behind us. As we were going through Mashpee, at the top of a hill, the car slid and we barely missed a tree that was on the edge of the road that must have been at least two feet in diameter. The car turned completely around and we went down this steep hill backwards slamming into a telephone pole that was on the edge of Mashpee lake (on the edge of the road). I know I flew up and hit the ceiling. I'm sure we all did. It was a sheer miracle none of us were hurt. When I turned around, the telephone pole was sticking up where the backseat should have been! Both of my shoes had come off and I was sitting on them. I guess it was a good thing though, that we hit the telephone pole. Otherwise we would have ended up in the lake.

Frankie Boyne barely missed us as he came sliding down the hill. After that our lights would not work. The boys were able to get the car out onto the highway again and Frankie Boyne was giving us a push, or a pull, I can't remember which, when we were stopped by the Mashpee Police. David got out and gave the policemen some kind of song and dance about being related to the Crosby Yacht Yard, and they let us go.

Howard never did actually ask me to marry him. It was cute the way he proposed. During one of our passionate kissing sessions during the summer of 1950, he would stop and say, "Now say Mrs. Howard Williams!" Of course I would whisper, "Mrs. Howard Williams." After another kiss he would say, "Now say it out loud!" - This happened several times. Then, by the end of the summer, before he went back to College (he was entering his third year at Boston College), when he found out I was enjoying the company of another young fellow, Jimmy Lebel, during the week while he was away at school, he decided I should have a ring. (Jimmy Lebel was a friend of my brothers. He had a steady girlfriend whom he also saw weekends. So during the week he would spend a lot of evenings at our house. We frequently went to the movies and bowling together. My mother and father even went along bowling with us once in a while. We had some fun times. I remember one evening when we went to the movies in Buzzard's Bay. On the way home we drove over a frozen lake in Marstons Mills and found a duck with its foot frozen in the ice. Of course Jimmy got out and rescued it! He gave it to me to hold and we took it home and put it in our cellar. When we walked in the house I found the bird had "messed" all over the front of my nice mouton lamb fur coat!!)

At any rate Howard decided I should have a ring. So two weeks before he went back to school we made arrangements to go to Boston to pick out the ring. It was a Saturday morning when he picked me up. We purchased the ring at Reagan-Kipp for $135.00. I picked it out in the window. Then my engagement was announced in the paper with a June 1951 wedding planned.

Now Howard has always had a lot of religion. He diplomatically explained to me that he wanted to be married inside the altar, so I would have to take lessons and become a Catholic. Well I was very meek and mild—and agreeable—in those days. And I loved Howard. So once again I was changing religions. First Baptist, then Methodist, and now I was becoming a Catholic.

Now, when I think back on it, I never did feel comfortable in that religion. I always felt as though I was in a foreign country. The service was always in LATIN and I never knew what they were saying, so I always said my own prayers! Also, I never got the satisfaction of going to church because I wanted to go. I was taught in that Church that I had to go, otherwise it was a venial sin! In the other two churches I always felt good about myself *because I went to Church because I wanted to go.* I always came out so enlightened.

My Married Years

The winter after we became engaged flew by quickly. Howard came home just about every week-end and we were very much in love. I converted to Catholicism and the wedding day finally arrived! The wedding itself was not without incident. We had a very strict and dictatorial priest in those days. His name was Father Buckley. He told us what time to be there and that we could not have a soloist!! On the day of the wedding, after I had walked down the aisle, I realized the person playing the organ was not the organist from the Catholic Church in Hyannis, whom I had hired, but the Sister (Nun). The Wedding March was not being played, but a "beat" similar. I never did actually hear what happened, but I heard via the grape vine, that Father Buckley did not allow the Wedding March to be played in that Church because it was written by an atheist!!

One day, a short while ago (this is forty five years later) I ran into the girl who was married just ahead of me. (I remember we had to wait for them to clear out before we could get into the church!) She said she didn't remember what had happened about the organist, but she did remember how upset they were when Father Buckley came out after the service and ordered them out of the parking lot as quickly as possible - or he was going to call the POLICE!! She said her mother reported him to the Archbishop.

One other incident!! In the middle of the service we heard a tap, tap, tap and paper rustling! The doors of the church had been left open. (It was a warm day.) A dog had entered the church and was walking down the aisle on the paper put down for the bride! It was one of those little hounds that walked crooked. You know, one of those dogs whose front legs don't line up with the back! When it reached the altar, the best man, Howard's brother Paul, had to leave and lead it out the side door.

It was a beautiful day and the reception was held outside in the yard at my parents' home. The only thing that happened out-of-the-way there was when I threw the bouquet. It stuck to my hand and landed up on the roof of the porch. Ed got the ladder and climbed up on the roof and threw it to my married sister Polly. I'm sure the other unmarried females were disappointed, but there wasn't much I could do about that!

Then we left for our honeymoon in New Hampshire.

(Oh, yes, the blue garter, which my sister-in-law, Barbara, gave me to put on I neglected to wear. And I went through the whole ceremony with six buttons undone on one wrist!!)

Our Reception Receiving Line
(Note Sam's Pond in background)

We went to New Hampshire on our honeymoon, staying at a different cabin each night. We visited the Polar Caves, the Flume, and the Old Man in the Mountain. On about the fourth morning Howard wanted to know if I was ready to head home. Well, to be honest with you, I was not only anxious to get back to our own little apartment to take up housekeeping and examine all of our gifts, but I was so constipated I couldn't eat another bite of food. The night before I could only eat about two bites of my delicious lobster salad. There wasn't room in my stomach for another bite. Every time I would go in to go to the bathroom, Howard would come in and want to know where I was, and that would be the end. I have always said since then that people should live together a few months—and then go on a honeymoon!

We had rented a two-room apartment up over Knute Carlson's garage on Old Mill Road where we lived for one year. It was cute. It had a good size living room with an open kitchen, the bath in the middle, and the bedroom off the kitchen on the back. We were very happy there, but I was terribly lonely there while Howard was away at school during the week. I was always so happy to see him walk up the driveway on Friday night.

Now I don't want to tell you what I am going to tell you next, but to be honest with myself I will.

I was a little bit spoiled when I got married. I wasn't the world's best cook, but I could fry things. One day I made a big pot of American Chop Suey, the way my mother always made it, which turned out super. (Made with salt pork, green

44

peppers, onions, hamburg, spaghetti, and tomato soup.) It was so delicious. But Howard ruined the whole meal! Without even tasting a bite, he doused his whole plate with ketchup!! I finished off my plate still priding myself with what a good job I had done. (It really was good, and even Howard said it was good!) But, after the meal, I was still upset about the ketchup incident, so I threw the rest of the whole pot out into the trash!!

Another time we were having steak for dinner. (I had just finished washing and waxing the kitchen floor.) Somehow Howard managed to let his steak slip off his plate and onto the floor. With that he took it over to the sink and proceeded to thoroughly wash it off with water! I took one look at him and said, "Well, if you are going to ruin your steak, I am not going to eat mine either!" With that I took mine over and put it in the trash. Howard always said he noticed how carefully I placed it in the trash, because I went over and took it out later and ate it, which was true!

There were other little incidents that happened such as those, too; but I soon learned that Howard was different from my family, and there wasn't anything I could do about it.

We had intended to wait a couple of years before having any children, but, wouldn't you know, I got pregnant the first month we were married. (Kevin was born nine months and two days after we were married. Bruce was born ten months and three weeks later, and David was born seventeen months later! Seven years later came Craig and Wayne!) Howard had brought this chart home from school which we faithfully abided by, but I still got pregnant.

I can hardly believe this, but a couple weeks ago, JANUARY 1996, an article was in the paper stating that Doctors have now determined exactly when a woman can get pregnant—four days before or at the beginning of her period!! (But that is too late for us!)

I continued to work the whole winter that first year we were married. Kevin was born on March 11th, and I received vacation pay while I was in the hospital. That was to be the last time I worked [outside the home] for twenty-two and a half years.

In the Spring a little birdie built a nest right outside our bedroom window where we could see right into it. It was so much fun watching that mother feed those wide open mouths. Then, one morning we got up and they were gone.

Well, that June Howard graduated from Boston College with honors, receiving his Bachelor's Degree in Math, and was offered a job at Curtis-Wright as an Engineer in Woodbridge, New Jersey. His brother Paul got him the position. We moved in with them for the summer that year in Ramsey, New Jersey. Howard rode back and forth to work with Paul. But then in September we bought our first car, a blue 1948 two-door Oldsmobile which we paid $1,500.00 for (used), and moved into our very own apartment in Wright Village in Lodi. Howard was able to walk to work from there.

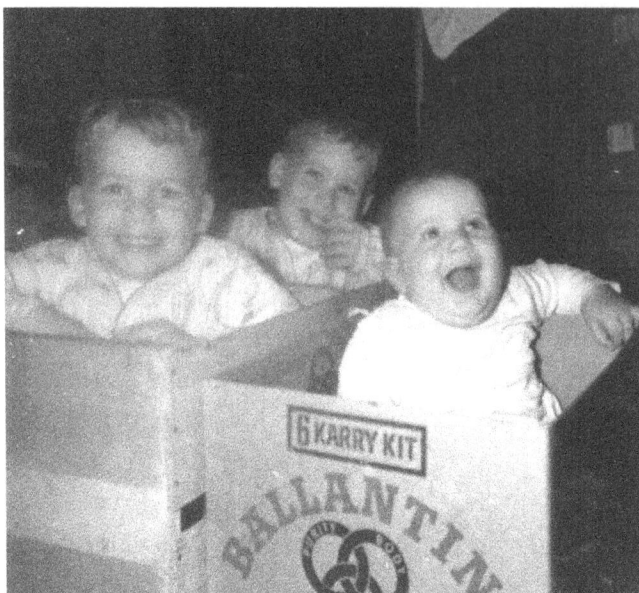

Kevin, Bruce and David

The one thing I remember about that place was how sweltering hot it was there in the summer! There wasn't any air conditioning and hardly a breath of air. Finally Howard MADE a window fan which helped some, but not much. (It made such a racket!)

We lived there for about two years and then we bought a house at 47 Beech Street in Ramsey, New Jersey, for $14,500.00. It was a very nice three-bedroom, one bath, living room, kitchen ranch with lots of trees in both the front and back yard. — — And a little bit of air!!

We were very happy there. We had nice neighbors and we had some good friends. With Anne and Bill Romas, and Thelma and Henry Lucky, we took dancing lessons and had lots of cook-outs and gatherings. Looking back on those years now, I would say they were pleasant years.

I can remember one year on Halloween, Anne Romas and I bundled our kids all up in strollers. It was cold that year. I had Kevin, Bruce and David, and she had Billy and we started trick or treating about 4:30 in the afternoon!! - With Anne and I stuffing our faces with candy. Now when I think back about it, it is embarrassing!

Another time I can remember we planned a ball game. Our street (or area) was going to play a girls team from my sister-in-law Barbara's development (MOMAR). Well, we got to the ball field and they were up first. I was pitcher. I think they got about 26 runs before we could get them out. Since I was the pitcher, I was the first one up. I got a real terrific hit, but on the way to first base, I got two wicked charley

46

horses—and that was the end of the game for me. I could hardly move my legs to get home, and I'm sure I was lame for several days! Needless to say they won the ball game. They had a girl on their team that I think was part man. She was the pitcher and I never saw any professional who was as good as she was. I'm sure anyone hit with one of her balls would have been dead.

It was while we were living in Ramsey that Bruce was so sick. It seems he was always running fevers - and we were always carting him to the Doctor. Even when we went to Cape Cod, he would look so pathetic, and I can remember letting him sleep on a pillow in the back seat or holding him in my arms all the way home.

He was about three years old and still wetting the bed. Howard and I would wake him up about eleven every night to take him to the bathroom, and then again about 2 AM trying to get him trained. Most of the time he wouldn't even wake up when we took him in.

Finally, one day I looked out the window where all of the other kids were playing and saw Bruce sound asleep on the ground. I knew then something was really wrong. We took him to the Doctor. He said his sedimentation rate was the highest he had ever seen and he had a heart murmur. He ordered him into the hospital immediately.

Bruce was in the hospital about a week. It was determined that he had bad tonsils and mononucleosis. They couldn't take the tonsils out right away because of his condition. He was put on penicillin the whole winter that year. Finally in the spring they were able to take his tonsils out. The Doctor said they were so rotten that when they put the clamps on them they just disintegrated.

Shortly after having his tonsils out, Bruce stopped wetting the bed and was normal in every way. (We had stopped trying to train him once we found out he was sick, and made up hospital beds for him.)

It was also while we were in New Jersey that Howard went to night school at the Newark College of Engineering, receiving his Master's Degree in Mechanical Engineering.

Well, we stayed in Ramsey for about three years, and then we decided we would like to be a little closer to Cape Cod. Curtis-Wright was moving to Pennsylvania and that was our opportunity. He applied and was accepted for a position at MIT's Lincoln Laboratory.

He accepted the position sometime during the summer, so we put the house on the market right away. We sold the house within three weeks, but a month or so later we learned the sale had fallen through. So it was put back on the market. Come September Howard had to leave and I was left behind to sell the house. He moved in with my sister, Polly, and her husband, Buddy Snyder, who lived on Sigourney Street in Lynn.

Fortunately for me the house wasn't on the market long until it sold again for $16,500.00. Once I was sure the sale was going through, I flew up to Boston to look for a house. After making two offers on a home in Acton, which were not accepted, we finally found a house in the process of being built at 547 Main Street in West Concord. I think we paid something like $19,500.00 for it. It was a ranch with three bedrooms, a dining room, living room, kitchen, bath, breezeway, and two-car garage. It was set a good distance back from the road with lots of trees in front and in back. We had a beautiful double-wide tarred driveway put in with a very nice turn-around up close to the garage so that we wouldn't have any trouble getting out into the street. Eventually we enclosed the breezeway and made a beautiful room out there with built-in bookcases. We also built an additional bedroom downstairs complete with raised floor and fully carpeted.

We had a nice back yard where we put a swing set and slide, and we had a nice drop-off on one side of the house where the kids had a great time sliding in the winter time. There was also a swamp nearby where the kids had a great time skating. The school bus picked them up right in front of the house.

When the kids got older, they all (older three) had paper routes. And they cleared people's driveways in the winter with a very elegant Toro snow blower which Howard bought. The neighbors were always very happy to pay them because we got some pretty deep snowstorms then. I would make them hot chocolate and Howard would deliver it to them along with doughnuts after they had been out a couple hours.

They had some good friends in the neighborhood, Joey and Jimmy Syiek, Freddy Tilton, Georgie Carlin, and Tommy and Chris Gibbs.

I can remember one time on Christmas Day when Tommy came over with a brand new pair of beautiful felt-lined gloves which his parents had given him as a gift. The kids played out in the yard in the snow for a long time. And then they came in the house to play downstairs. Tommy's gloves were soaked. I don't remember who put the gloves on top of the heating vent downstairs to dry, but I do know that when it came time to go home, one of the kids went to get the gloves. I will never forget the look on Tommy's face!! We were all in shock! I am sure he was afraid he was going to get the devil when he got home, but the gloves had shrunk to the size of a three year old's hand. (Tommy must have been about 12.) Over the years that has been mentioned so many times in our family and we always get a big laugh out of it, even though it really wasn't funny.

Another thing that happened while we were in Concord: a little mixed-breed dog followed Wayne home from a friend's house one day. I was sure he was paying a lot of attention to it! I told Wayne he couldn't keep the dog. I did not want any animals; I figured we had enough kids to care for. And we lived on the Main Street. Well, the little dog wouldn't leave. We inquired around, but nobody knew who the little dog belonged to. He slept outside the door that night on the door step. The next morning he watched Wayne get on the school bus, and was right there when he got off the bus at noon. He followed him everywhere he went. Well, of course, Wayne had to give him water and food. And the following night he was invited into the house to sleep. We named him "Sandy".

He had a great time at our house. The kids all loved him. We didn't restrict the dog at all. He was allowed to go in and out at will, because he really wasn't ours. We didn't know whom he belonged to.

About three or four weeks later, I was on the Emerson Hospital Rummage Sale Committee, and that was the day of the sale, so I had to leave home early. I put a big ham bone in the back yard to keep the dog busy, and then I took Wayne up the street to get on the bus at the neighbors.

I don't remember whether Wayne got off the school bus at the neighbors that day, or I came home early. But I do remember when I came home that day that Wayne couldn't wait to tell me that the little dog had been hit by a car that morning in front of the Syiek house. He said the Police came, but he didn't know where Sandy was [taken] because he had to get on the bus. So I called the Police and they gave me the name of the Veterinarian's Hospital where he had been taken.

So Wayne and I hopped in the car and went to the hospital. They took us into a room where he was in a topless low cage. When the little dog saw us he put his paw on the wire for us to touch. Dried blood was running from his nose. He had been sedated so he was not in any pain. The Doctor said he had a concussion and a broken back, and he wasn't sure he would ever be able to walk again. I said, "Well, maybe we should have him put to sleep." The Doctor said, "Is that what you want?" And I said, "Yes." But I told the Doctor I wanted to be with the dog when he was put to sleep. I told Wayne to wait in the waiting room, and then I was led into another room. They brought in the dog on a small stretcher. About the only thing he could move was his eyes. (It must have been an effort for him to move his paw that one time.) I stroked the little dog to let him know I was there. The Doctor filled the syringe and then he turned to me and said, "Is this little dog yours?" I said, "Yes." He said, "Now you must raise your hand and swear the little dog is yours." So I raised my hand and said, "I swear this little dog is mine!!" With that he put the needle into his leg and it was all over instantly. The little dog never flinched or moved a muscle. I know because my hand was on his body. (The only thing that happened was that his bladder let go and the urine flowed out onto the table.)

I have always regretted the fact that I didn't take Wayne in with me. I have never regretted the fact that I did what I did, because at the time there were horrible pictures in the paper of animals being experimented on and I didn't want to have that worry! I know for a fact that Sandy went to heaven!! The next week we got a bill for $90.00 which we paid.

We lived at this residence for ten years. They were busy years. Craig and Wayne were both born at Emerson Hospital in Concord. Not only were two additional children born at this location, but Howard decided to go back to school. He spent four years going to night school three nights a week, getting his Juris Doctor in Law with honors in 1963 [from Boston College].

Between school, studying, Boy Scouts, Little League and various other events, it was a full life. I did manage to get on a bowling team with other mothers in the area. It was during this hectic period that I stopped going to church.

All of our vacations during this ten year period, with the exception of two, included all of the children. One of the two was when Howard was attending a convention in Miami. My mother came up and stayed with the five children so that I could go. We stayed at the Fontainebleau, and had a great time.

The other was a week vacation in Fort Lauderdale, Florida, when we took Howard's mother along. (She had never been to Florida.) Once again my poor mother took over the duties of caring for the children.

All of the other vacations were spent going to New Hampshire, Maine, and Cape Cod. The New Hampshire and Maine trips were usually long weekend ventures. Howard had purchased 420 acres of land in Thorndike, Maine, when we first moved to Concord. He paid $2,200.00 for it and sold it fifteen years later for $75,000.00. We would go there once or twice a year to check on the land, taking along a Coleman Burner and having a cook-out on the property. I would always take along a frying pan and we would stop and buy big thick steaks to cook which were always so delicious, along with potato salad, cole slaw, and a big delicious cake.

I can remember one time when Wayne was little and couldn't swim. He slipped off the edge of the deep end of the pool at one of the hotels we were staying at in Waterville. When his little head popped out of the water he reached out and grabbed the rope which was strung along the edge of the pool. I thought that was pretty clever. We always looked for motels with pools when we went north.

Another time a friend of Howard's at work told him he could stay at his place in Maine for a week. All we had to do was pay for the electricity. He said it was 90% complete and it was on a lake. Well, we were all enthused and we planned to stay for a week. We loaded down our Chevy Impala taking a carriage for Craig to sleep in. (Wayne wasn't here yet.) We stopped in a town just before we got there and bought a lot of groceries. We stopped at a Church Bake Sale along the way and bought a huge cake.

Finally we arrived at the two-story house which was in a remote area. The first thing we had to do was turn on the electricity. The fuse box was outside and was so full of caterpillars that Howard had to use a long stick to clear them away before we could see to turn it on. Then we discovered that we had to go buy fuses! After that we walked into the area off the kitchen where we were to turn on the gas. Now I don't want to tell you this, because this was just plain STUPID!! But I thought I smelled gas so I ordered everybody out of the house, and then I lit a match outside—and walked inside with my arm way out in front!! Fortunately, nothing happened. The sink was full of dirty cups and dishes where someone had eaten and enjoyed hot chocolate. The fireplace had an eight foot long log sticking out of it. (Burned on the end that was in the fireplace.) And the 90% complete house only had 2 x 4s upstairs separating the bedrooms ! !

That night, after we got into bed, Howard had to go downstairs to turn the lights off. Well, wouldn't you know, Howard would stub his toe badly on his way back up the unfinished cement stairs leading to the bedrooms. Of course the kids thought that was funny. Finally we all got settled into bed which was fun, because we could all talk to each other and the kids could hear Howard's stomach growling from the next room!! But that is not the end to this unusual story! About two minutes later, about 1000 mosquitoes descended upon our upstairs bedrooms. Fortunately I had brought along a net for Craig's carriage, but the rest of us had to suffer. We spent the night listening to the zzzzz's, and every time one stopped, we'd wait to see who got bitten! We finally all fell asleep (from exhaustion I'm sure) with sheets over our heads.

At 5 AM we were awakened by the loud motor boats speeding back and forth on the lake right outside our window! But, needless to say, we had already made up our minds, we were heading home that very day. But, and that's a big BUT, before we did, the kids wanted to go swimming. They had only been swimming about twenty minutes when David came out of the water and I saw blood running down his leg. I called him over and saw what I thought was a worm sticking out of his leg!! Then we noticed they were all over the place there. They were blood suckers!! So the rest of the kids were ordered out of the water for inspection. We found a few hanging on them. Even after we got in the car to head home, we found one crawling on Bruce's foot. The three older boys have never forgotten that vacation. They refer to it as the trip to Blood Sucker Island!

Usually when we took a week's vacation, we went to Cape Cod. Our poor parents again!! Howard never thought anything about it, but I always felt a little bit guilty about piling in on our families with all of our kids. After Craig and Wayne were born, I usually stayed over at my mother's with them and Howard stayed over at his mother's with the three older ones. They lived almost across the street from each other between two [Sam's and Joshua's] ponds.

Even though they only lived about a mile and one half from the ocean, the kids usually preferred to spend most of their time swimming at Joshua's Pond where there was a raft and a life guard, and fishing on Sam's Pond where Howard's mother owned right down to the water and had a row boat. The kids had great times, and I'm sure Howard and I did also; but when I think back now on those years, I think of those ten years as the "wearing" years. They were busy, busy, busy.

After Howard graduated from Law School and passed the Massachusetts Bar Exam, he applied for a position at a few law firms. He had one offer in Boston as a Patent Attorney, but the salary was too low; so he started a practice of his own, in addition to [keeping] his job at The MITRE Corporation. So now, in addition to all my other duties, I became a receptionist and secretary, doing all of the typing.

Howard, his mother, me, Buddy and Pally and my mother

It was during this phase of our busy life [1968] that Howard came home from work one day and told us all at the dinner table about this tremendous job offer he had in Tampa, Florida. Much to Howard's surprise, all of our ears perked up - and we ALL said we wanted to go. Howard said he just couldn't believe it! The next day he called his friend in Florida and told him he was interested.

Howard went for his interview in Tampa and a few days later received his letter of acceptance. A week or two later airline tickets were received for us both to return to look the place over and check on housing. Once again my mother came up to stay with the children. I was elated. On my first trip ever to Florida I knew that was the place for me. I was never one to appreciate the cold weather, and heat never bothered me.

Fortunately for me, we had renovated the whole house within the past couple years. I had newly papered every room. We were able to put the house on the market right away.

Over the next couple months we managed to finish up all of Howard's law work and he left the first week in April 1968 for Florida, staying in a tiny apartment in St. Petersburg by himself.

Oh yes, I forgot to tell you one thing that was unusual that happened when we lived in Concord. When Craig was about four years old we piled all five kids in the wagon to go to look at a boat that was for sale. Howard had seen an ad in the paper. On the way we stopped at Victory Market to let Kevin run in to get something. (I don't remember what he went in for.) The rest of us stayed in the car. While he was in there Craig said, "Let me out. I want to get some gum." So we let Craig out. Then Kevin returned and got in the car and we drove off!! It wasn't until we got about six miles away that Howard looked in the rear view mirror and said, "Where's Craig?" Then I remembered, "Oh, my God, he got out to get gum." Well, I thought I would have a heart attack. That was the longest ride back that I have ever taken in my whole life! Fortunately for us Craig had sense enough to stand in front of the store and wait, which is where we found him when we returned. I have often wondered if he watched the car drive away and what he was thinking!!

We had some good times in Concord, too. We were very close with three other families in the neighborhood. They were Marge and Joe Ryan, Agnes and Joe Syiek, and Ethel and George Carlin. We had some tremendous fun time parties with them, especially on Halloween. I can remember one Halloween Party when Howard wore my bathing suit with a long hair, brown and beige blanket wrapped around his waist. He went as a caveman. He found an old piece of tree out in the yard with a huge knot on the end of it which he carried. The party was at the Carlins.

When we stopped to pick up the Syieks on the way, Howard saw a bunch of bananas on their counter; so he grabbed a bunch and hung them on his belt. Then he had a wad of chewed up gum sticking out of one nostril!! Why we just laughed ourselves silly that night. I went as a witch.

Howard always was BIG on Halloween costumes. I remember one year when the kids had a Cub Scout Halloween party. David wore a bonnet with a blouse and skirt, with a pair of shorts underneath. Howard had sewn a piece of pink crepe paper around the bottom of the shorts so that they would look like pantaloons. Then he carried a cane with a ribbon on it and a sign that said PIDDLE-LO-BEEP! ! Bruce went as Aunt Jemima. He had great big red lips drawn on his face. His face had been blackened and he wore a red handkerchief tied around his head with the knot in front. He had BIG balloon boobs underneath one of my old red cotton dresses. He wore gloves and carried an ironing board!! We always had such fun doing these things. But I have to admit, most of the ideas were Howard's.

That's Howard in back with the tree stump.
I'm the witch!

The last weekend Howard was home before he went to Florida the Syieks called and said they wanted to take us out to dinner. Well, the night of the dinner, we heard this CLANG-CLANG-CLANG coming down the street, and lo and behold, it came right into our driveway!! It was the Syieks coming to pick us up. Their muffler had fallen down and was being dragged on the street. Of course, Howard offered to drive. But Joe wouldn't hear of it; THEY were taking US to dinner! Well, we laughed all the way to Russo's in Maynard. Then with sparks flying and CLANG-CLANG-CLANG we laughed all the way home.

Some other good times I should tell you about were when we went crabbing on Cape Cod. We would take the car and some nets and go to Mashpee, where Howard's Uncle Jesse Murray had a cabin and where Howard visited often as a child. We would open the trunk of the car and fill it right up with crabs. When it was full we would take them home, where his mother would have a couple pots of water boiling. Then we would eat them outside, in back, where she had a picnic bench. I can remember one time when I ate thirteen crab!! (That's hard to believe, now.)

Well, back to our departure from Concord. When school let out in June, I took the five children and left for Cape Cod for the summer. Once again the three older boys stayed at Howard's mother's. And I and the two younger ones stayed at my mother's house. (Howard was temporarily settled in his tiny apartment in St.

Petersburg.) The Concord house had been sold in early May and all of the furniture left to go into storage in Florida. Before we left for Cape Cod, Howard came home for the weekend to help close the place up. (The actual closing, passing of title, on the property took place in July, by our attorneys, without either of us having to be present.)

Next came our jaunt to Florida. The summer passed by quickly (or so it seems now). Then the six of us took the bus to Boston and boarded the plane at Logan for Tampa. We were to stay at two motel units on Clearwater Beach while our new house was being built at 313 Leeward Island on Island Estates in Clearwater, located on the water on a finger right off the Causeway to Clearwater Beach. Each unit had a living room, small kitchen, bedroom and bath. The three older boys slept in one unit, with three beds in the fairly large bedroom. Craig and Wayne slept in our unit in the living room on two couches (or cots) which had been put in for that purpose. Howard and I had the bedroom.

The units, or I should say, the whole FANWILL Complex was in sort of a run-down condition, but we thought we could put up with it for the short while we should be there!! And it was the best Howard could do. He got turned down at several others, but I'm sure it was because we had so many kids. I really didn't blame them.

At any rate, this jaunt to Florida turned out to be a fiasco. We ended up living in those run-down quarters for six months ! ! [David: we kids loved it there.]

But before I go on, I want to stop and tell you about the hurricane we had while we were there on the beach. I don't remember which month it was in, (Howard says September) but I do remember we were all forewarned. We had been listening to the radio all day. At five o'clock that night it was decided that Clearwater Beach should be evacuated. Trucks with loud speakers rode up and down the roads, telling everyone to get out. Well, I don't know where our judgment was, but we, and several others, decided to stay. That night about seven o'clock The National Guard came around and took all of our names. (We always joked about it later and said they took our names for the OBITUARY column.)

Well, the storm arrived all right. The rain came down in buckets. And the winds howled ferociously. Before long, water was dripping from the ceiling light sockets. During the middle of it all Howard and Kevin went out to move the car. They decided it might be a little safer beside the Gas Station Building next door. They pulled in just in time to see the large plate glass in the window in front being blown out! At some time, I remember one of our neighbors in an upper floor unit coming down to see if we wanted to come up with them. (We didn't.) Well, it was a long night with all the howling and dripping, and without any electricity, but we survived. And we did manage to sleep some.

The next morning we were all up early. There were still humongous waves on the ocean, so Howard and the three older boys decided to go swimming!! They were having so much fun body surfing on those huge waves, until one big wave brought Howard in and dumped him on the shore, taking the skin off his nose. That was the end of the swimming!!

We learned later that the roof had fallen in on the school where they had taken the people from Clearwater Beach. I don't remember how many, or if any, were injured.

Wayne

Another incident that happened while we were staying on Clearwater Beach. We were only there a few days when it was time for Wayne to enter first grade. That first week school was only in session mornings so that the teacher could schedule appointments to meet with each student and parent (or parents) in the afternoon. Wayne's appointment was at two o'clock. Well, that first day, school got out at 11:30. Wayne came home and had lunch and then asked if he could go to the Community [Youth] Center, which was only a few [hundred] yards down the road. I said, "Yes, but be sure to be home by 1:30, because we have to be at the school." He said, "O.K." Well, come 1:30, - NO WAYNE, so I rode down to the Community Center, but couldn't find him. Come two o'clock, NO WAYNE; Come 2:30 and three o'clock, NO WAYNE!!

By then I was worried sick, so I called the Clearwater Police Department. They came to the apartment and asked all kinds of questions, wanted a picture, and took a description and put out an ALL POINTS BULLETIN to be on the look-out for Wayne. I guess they scoured the area that day, but it wasn't until after five o'clock that afternoon that they spotted him coming over the Clearwater Causeway on his bicycle with another young fellow about eleven years old. They notified me right away. I guess they had an awful time getting him into the cruiser. He wanted to ride home himself, but they finally arrived with Wayne in the back seat and his bicycle in the trunk. I was so relieved to see him! (Wouldn't you know, Howard was out of town.) All I could think of was, what will I ever do when it gets dark!!

Well, Wayne said this fellow was going to show him something. So he took him over the Causeway to Maas Bros. (both on bikes) where the kid stole some things from the store and bought him a drink. Wayne said he had to stay with the fellow because he didn't know his way back! He said he kept telling the fellow his mother would be "wearied".

Pink Shirt, Blue Shorts

CLEARWATER -- Five-year-old Wayne Williams, 657 Mandalay Ave., led the Clearwater Police Department on a merry chase most of yesterday afternoon.

Wayne was supposed to have returned home at noon so his mother could take him to school to meet his new teacher. He never showed up.

At about 2 p.m. she called the Clearwater police.

She reported that her son, wearing a pink shirt, blue shorts, and white tennis shoes and riding a bicycle, was missing.

Officers immediately started combing the Clearwater Beach area.

At about 5:30, Patrolman R. D. McManus spotted the youngster riding home along Clearwater Memorial Causeway. McManus put Wayne, his bicycle, pink shirt, blue shorts, and white tennis shoes in the patrol car and took him straight home.

Now for the FIASCO! The new home which we contracted for in early June was to be built on our lot at 313 Leeward Island with completion promised by the early part of September. It was to be built exactly like the model. We were assured that everything would be the same except for maybe an item now and then that had been "discontinued." But we were told not to worry, "It is usually only a light fixture or something."

Well, when we arrived the end of August, nothing had been done. The grass was still growing all over our property!! By the time construction did commence, we had all kinds of problems. We managed to get many of them corrected along the way. Some of the changes we accepted because, although they were different, they still looked nice. But two of the problems we absolutely refused to accept. One was the replacement of the Lumidor sliding glass doors with inferior ones made by another manufacturer. We stood firm on that issue. I called the Lumidor Factory in Miami and talked to the Vice President and was assured they were still in business and the doors were still available.

The other item we refused to accept was the woodwork. Our woodwork was to be stained the same soft shade as the model with the grain showing. They had used the wrong wood for stain in our house, so they painted it a dark brown and went over it with varnish!

We ordered Clearwater Beach Bank where we were getting our mortgage to NOT give them any more mortgage money until we told them to do so. (It was a construction mortgage.) A few weeks later I went down to the bank to tell them to continue to hold the money, and found that, without our permission, they had gone ahead and given them ALL of the mortgage money. Fortunately for us, we still owed them $6,000.00 Plus, out of our own pocket, for extras that we had done. We refused to pay.

The builder had given us several different move-in dates. Each time we notified our moving company. Each time we had to cancel. Finally our moving company got fed up. They said our furniture was on the truck and they were NOT moving them into the warehouse again! So we ended up getting permission from the builder to store the furniture in our two-car garage. But then the builder changed the lock on the garage so that we could NOT get in. The upshot of the whole mess was that we broke into the garage and MOVED INTO the house without permission!!

I won't go into all of the threats that were made after that!! It was a mess. But there wasn't anything they could do about it because it was OUR property. They ended up suing us and putting a lien on our property.

The first attorney we had was recommended by Scotty Peak. -Green, I think his name was, but he turned out to be in the enemy camp. We were all set to go to court when one of his cohorts called us and advised us that we should go ahead and settle. Howard wasn't home, so I did the responding. He said he didn't think we would win. To which I replied, "I can't imagine any court in the world NOT finding for us." He said, "Well, it all depends on the mood of the judge." To which I said, "Well, if you people feel like that, then we should be having a jury trial." He said, "It's too late now to have a jury trial." I said, "Well, how could Mr. Green get us into a rut like this?" He said, "You know he is charging you $125.00 an hour for his time, including this phone call!" (We had been talking 20 minutes to 1/2 hour.) I said, "No, he isn't." He said, "Yes, he is." I said, "No, he isn't." I said, "Mr. Green, when we questioned him about his fees, assured us that whatever we had to pay, we would be happy with." The next day we received a notice in the mail that they were withdrawing from our case. We should find another attorney.

Well, thanks to [friend and neighbor] Alvie Prokes, she recommended Attorney Alex Finch. He was the only one with enough backbone and big enough in town to take on that organization. No matter how large the Corporation, or how difficult the problem, he was ready. He wasn't afraid of anyone.

It turned out to be a long drawn out court battle. It took about three years before it was straightened out. But in the end, thanks to Alex Finch, we won both the Court Case and the Appeal. And we didn't have to pay one additional penny!

Despite the law suit and all the troubles we had with Imperial Homes, those were happy years for me. I have always been happy in Florida. The house was so big and beautiful. The most beautiful of all the houses we have ever owned. It had four bedrooms (the master bedroom being 28 feet long), living room, kitchen, dining room, three bathrooms, a large Florida Room, laundry room, two-car garage, and a screened-in porch across the back which was only 20 feet from the water. The mullet use to jump into the sailboat which we had. One morning we were awakened by some cries for "help." It was Craig. He was over the seawall and the ladder had floated away that we used when the tide was low.

Once again we made some good friends at this location also. There was Richard and Lois Cardin, Dick and Alvie Prokes, Kay and Al Griffith and Jim and Pat Caterina. They were our everyday companions.

Each day I would do the housework, deliver kids to school, or go shopping in the morning. After lunch I would always go to the Snoop Shop during the week and stay most all afternoon, or until the kids came home from school. There were always several women there where we discussed all the gossip and news. I did a lot of gold-leafing and made many nice ceramic wall ornaments, plaques and figurines.

Evenings were just like heaven in Clearwater. - Even in the summer. Many nights around 9:30, Howard and I would get on our bikes and ride all over the island. It was so peaceful. We'd watch people fishing on the little bridges between the islands.

Now for the fish story which I must not forget to tell you. One afternoon Howard and I were out in the yard by the sea wall. We looked down and there was a fish between two rocks (the tide was low). It had human eyes with what looked like eyelashes, and ears that stuck out like Mickey Mouse's. It was looking straight up at us—right into our eyes.

I said, "Quick, Howard, get the net. Nobody will ever believe this!" Lois Cardin came along while Howard was getting the net, so she was able to see it. But then Howard came back. He was being very cautious, but as soon as he put the net out over the water, there was a SWISH and the fish was gone, leaving a little bit of murky water in its place. I always felt bad that we didn't catch that fish, because now we don't know what we saw!

After living for two years in what I called "heaven," things did not begin to sound so good at the company where Howard was employed. They had lost several of their government contracts at MacDill Air Force Base, and people were leaving. A few months later he came home one night and said he was going to fly over to Miami the next day to resign. That really wasn't a shock to me, but it was a disappointment. I really didn't want to leave this area. Fortunately for Howard, he phoned his old company and they were able to take him back. Not in Bedford [MA] though, but in McLean, Virginia.

That Fall, October 1970, with David a Junior, Bruce a Senior, and Kevin enrolled at the University of South Florida, and the two younger ones in grade school, Howard left for Virginia. The house was still tied up in Court.

At the end of the school year the three older boys went to Cape Cod for the summer. The two younger ones and I spent the summer in Virginia with Howard. By now the law suits were over and the house was clear to sell, but because it was David's last year, and because he was on the first string football team (all three boys played football at Clearwater), I thought he would be disappointed if we moved him, so I stayed behind for another year.

We managed to survive without Howard that year, but it was during this year that Wayne skipped school. He was in the fourth grade, no less. (I can hardly believe that a child of mine would skip school in Grammar School!) His teacher called me about 3:20 that day to tell me that Wayne was not in school that day. He was just walking in the door. I couldn't believe what I was hearing. So I said, "Wayne, this is the teacher on the phone, and she says you were not in school today." He said, "Yes, I was. I went in late and sat in the back seat." The teacher said, "Believe me, Mrs. Williams, he was not here."

I don't remember how the conversation ended, but I do know I was more inclined to believe Wayne. (Isn't that awful?) It wasn't until a week or so later, when a Real Estate man stopped by to see if I was lonesome!! that Wayne confessed. The Real Estate man said that Wayne had spent the day over around his office, and told him that his father was living up in Washington!! Wayne had to admit then that he had skipped school because he had to give an oral book report that day and "I didn't want to stand up in front of all those kids."

The school year soon ended. The house in Clearwater sold in June 1972 for $62,500.00. (We had about $42,000.00 invested in it.) Howard arrived and once again was there to help out while all of our furniture was loaded on the van to go into storage while we looked for a place in Virginia to buy.

I will never forget how sad I was being driven down Leeward Island away from that beautiful home forever. I had never been attached to any of our other houses like that.

The two younger ones and I stayed at Howard's small apartment in McLean. The older boys were on the Cape. We started looking for a house to buy right away, but after a couple weeks it looked fruitless, so we rented a home in Greenbriar.

Then I became ill. My eyesight was terrible. I felt as though I was looking through cheesecloth all the time. Bubbles were popping in the top of my head, and I had no energy. I just felt miserable all the time. The Doctors ran all kinds of tests on me. I had all kinds of X-rays, a brain scan, dye placed in my kidneys, and an upper and lower GI series with nothing found other than hypoglycemia (low blood sugar). I was sure I was dying.

A couple months after we had been at Greenbriar, we went for a ride one day in McLean. We rode down Great Falls Street and there at Scotts Run was a sign "House For Sale." So we rode down Scotts Run and there on both sides of the road on Box Elder Court were two houses for sale with "OPEN HOUSE" on both. Howard said, "Do you want to go in?" I said, "Yes," even though we weren't looking for a house right now. We were locked into a year's lease. We walked through both homes and liked one very much. It had a two-car garage and was $3,000.00 cheaper than the other one. They were asking $79,000.00 for the other one. The one we liked with the garage was $76,000.00.

We told the Realtor that we liked the house but we couldn't buy right now because we were locked into the rental. I liked the house but I didn't give it much thought after that, because I was still sick and thought I was dying! Well, two days later Howard came to me and said he was going to make an offer on that home: $72,500.00, take it or leave it. No counter offers. That was what he told the Realtor and that was what the Realtor told the sellers.

They took it.

I'm not sure now whether we got our security deposit back, but they did allow us to get out of the lease. I think they rented it right away.

We moved into our new home at 7506 Box Elder Court shortly after Thanksgiving [1972]. A few days before the closing Howard rode by one day in time to see the old lady of the house throwing a huge pile of firewood over the fence into the yard of the German diplomat neighbors!! They weren't going to leave us one extra thing! All of the light bulbs, and even the door knocker, were gone.

We did have some nice neighbors though. Gunn McKay, a Congressman from Utah, and his family moved into the house across the street. Diagonally across from us was the home of Dr. Cecil Jacobson, now known as the "sperm doctor." They claim he fathered 72 children! [Google it] I always did feel bad about that, because they were good neighbors and actually a lovely family. They were good to us and they were good to our children.

A8   Thursday, Feb. 27, 1992   The Philadelphia Inquirer

Doctor says he impregnated women with his sperm but it wasn't wrong

Fair Comment

Insight ·   *April 6, 1992*

All Jokes Aside, Fertility Case Raises Some Serious Issues

By Suzanne Fields

We've seen the porcine face of the promiscuous fertility doctor on the front pages, his double chin jiggling like a bowl of jelly. But we were all a little surprised when he was convicted on 52 counts of fraud and perjury.

We've laughed, a little perversely, about the man the New York tabloids called "the sperminator" and imag- ined offspring with his distinctive looks decorating the Northern Virginia landscape for the next 50, 60, 70 years.

Fantasy scenarios leap to mind, half brother meeting half sister with desire under the elms, falling in love, never suspecting the attraction of like to like is genetically based. (Surely Sidney Sheldon is already working on the book that will be the miniseries.)

I can remember one time when Howard wasn't feeling well. I called him over, and he came with his little black bag and checked him out. He said he didn't think it was anything to worry about. His heart, lungs, and whatever else he checked were fine.

Another time he brought Wayne home from Boy Scouts and came in the house and told us he should be checked because he had high blood pressure.

I never will understand how their lives turned from such bliss to such agony. I'm sure he didn't think he was doing anything wrong.

Next door to Cecil lived Bill and Jane Daly. She became one of my closest friends. We still keep in touch to this day.

And I must not forget to mention our good friends, Eva and Earl Johnson, in this area either. We played cards and went out to dinner every Friday night with them for a good many years, before they packed up and moved away to Orlando, Florida. Now we visit each other periodically. We met them at a social at the Rotunda in McLean.

Now to get back on track! I was still very sick when we moved into the house, and everything I did was an effort. The house needed so much done to it. It had hardwood floors throughout, except for the family room, but the house was so cold. So the first thing we did was to go pick out carpeting (at Sears) with heavy padding underneath which we had installed wall to wall in the dining room, living room, hallways, and all of the bedrooms. We thought that would make the house warmer.

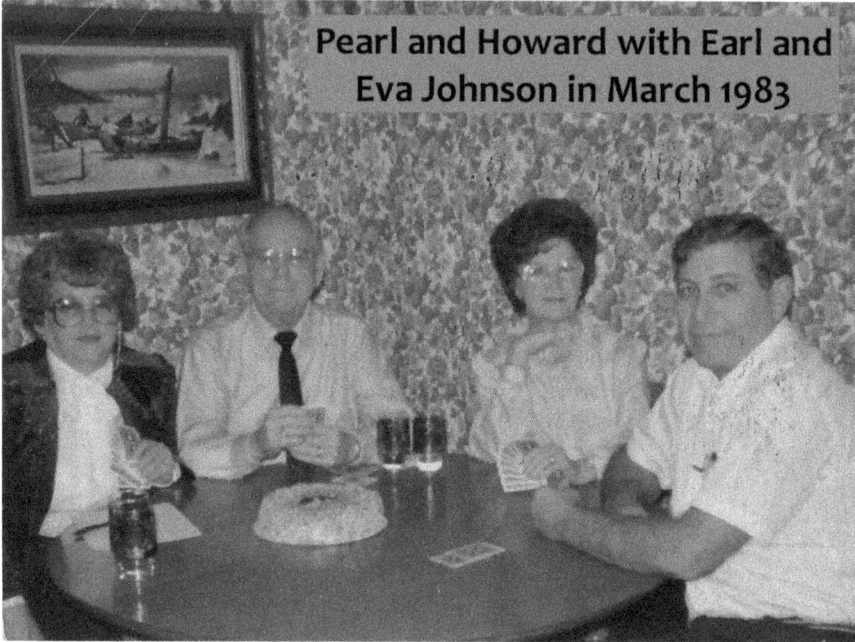

Pearl and Howard with Earl and Eva Johnson in March 1983

Then, because I was still sure I was dying, I wanted to get the house decorated as fast as I could, so that Howard wouldn't have any trouble selling it, if he had to, after I was gone. So gradually I picked out wallpaper, and hung about three strips a day, until all eight rooms were papered that needed paper. The family room, bedroom downstairs, and rec-room downstairs were all paneled.

Over the months curtains were put up, with drapes ordered for the living room and master bedroom, and the house began to take shape. I didn't realize it at the time, but I was beginning to take shape too!! One day I woke up, about a year and one half after we had been there, and I realized my eye sight was back to normal. I think now that my whole problem was psychological—moving from that big beautiful Florida home. Even the air in Clearwater was tonic to me. But nobody will ever convince me I wasn't sick. I know I was.

Our Family Pictures

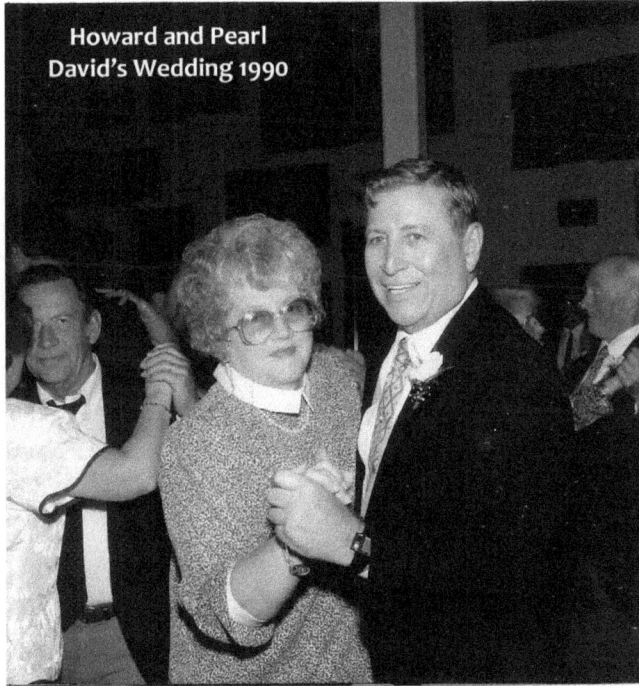

Howard and Pearl
David's Wedding 1990

Kevin and Linda   2000

Bruce and Chris at David's 1990 wedding. Their children, Rebecca and Jonathan.

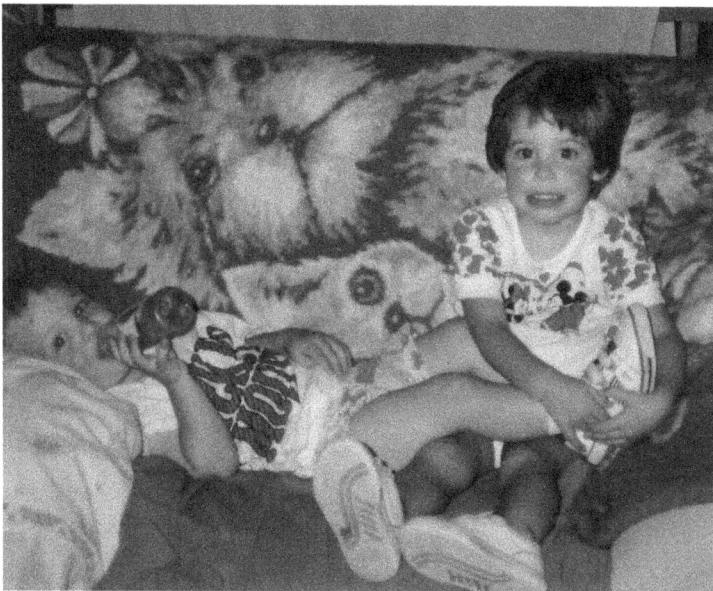

Our Family Pictures

David and Jennifer and their kids, Spencer and Oliver

Nov 1990

Nov. 4, 1998

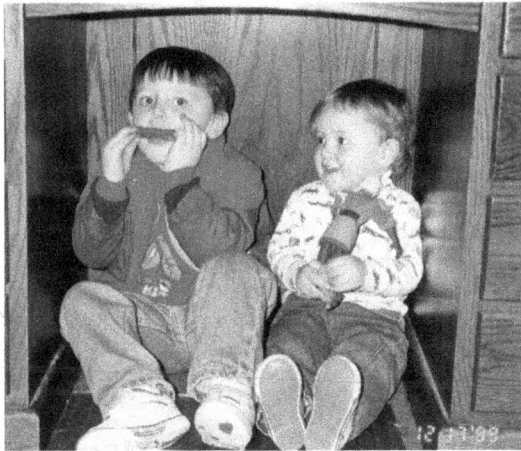

Craig and Mandy with their kids, Christina and Michael

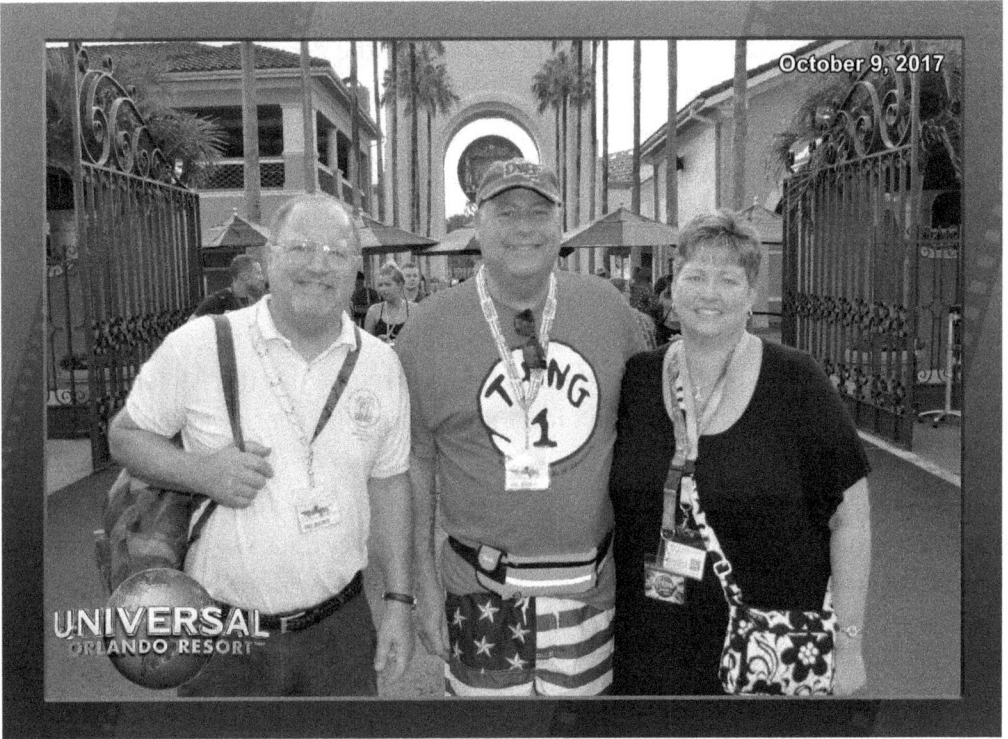

David with Wayne and Bridget

Twenty-five years after enlisting and serving his hitch in the Army, Wayne would discover that he had an adult daughter by a previous flame. And now he has a biological granddaughter too.

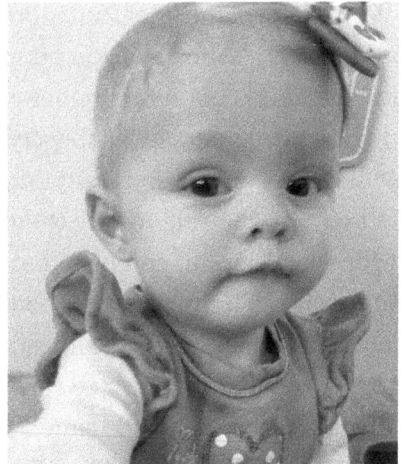

Dana Patrick and daughter Freya Halley.

My Work Years

After a couple years of living in McLean, despite the good company of Jane Daily, I had this yearning to get out and get myself a job. I had always admired people who worked. They seemed to know so much, filling out forms, etc. And I knew so little!!

So one day I told Howard that I was going to apply for a part-time job at the Hecht Co. The two younger children were now in Junior High School so there wasn't any reason I couldn't.

To make a long story short, there wasn't an office job available, so I accepted a position on the terminal in the housewares department from 9 to 2 PM Monday through Friday. I was there about three weeks, when one day the Personnel Manager went by, and I said, "Don't forget me for an office job, will you?" She said, "That I will definitely do."

And that very afternoon I was called in to help find errors on the tapes. From there they made me assistant to the Credit Manager. My desk was right outside the Credit Manager's office. Her name was Aggie Parks. She was one of those little power houses who wasn't afraid to stand up to anybody! I'm sure she was less than five feet tall and weighed less than 100 lbs.

One day a short time later a lady came in to me and said that she had ordered three pair of men's undershorts and three tee shirts from the store. (At the time, no delivery charges were made on any order over $6.00.) They were out of the underpants, so they sent her the tee shirts and charged her for the delivery. She wanted the delivery charges removed. Well, I didn't see any problem with that, so I wrote up a voucher, explaining the situation and requesting the delivery charges be removed, and put it on the Credit Manager's desk.

Well, a short time later, out stormed the Credit Manager and lit into me, but good. She said, "Who gave you permission to do this? You don't have the authority to do that." And I don't remember what else she said, but I do know that by the time she finished I was uncontrollably crying. Big tears were flowing down my face and I couldn't stop. I got up and went into the Personnel Manager's office to tell her that I wasn't going to be able to stay there, but she wasn't in. It was about 4:30. I couldn't wait for five o'clock to come so that I could go home. The crying continued and I could hardly see to drive myself home. When I walked in the house, Howard wanted to know what happened?!! I told him, and that I was going to quit. He said, "I think you'd better if you are going to take it that hard."

The next morning I had calmed down some, but I did go in to the Personnel Manager and tell her that unless she could find me another position I was going to leave. I told her that the Credit Manager didn't want someone to help her, she wanted someone she could walk on. She said she understood and she would see what she could do. About two weeks later she called me in and told me they had created a position for me in the Furniture Department as Customer Service Representative. I stayed there for over two years loving every minute of it.

Then I was called in one day and told that the Credit Manager was retiring and they asked me to take the position. I stayed there for another two plus years. It was a responsible position. I had unlimited authorization. Some of the fur sales were a little "scary." I remember one time when I took a check for $2,600.00 (or $3,600.00—I don't remember which). I was called a couple days later and told the check had bounced!! The next day I was told the woman had taken the coat back to another store to wait to get the funds transferred. I learned later that the clerk there sold it back to her for $26.00!! (That was corrected also.) I guess when one thing goes wrong, everything goes wrong!

One day a woman employed at the Central Intelligence Agency came in. She had sent in a check for $840.00 and was given credit for $84.00, which I straightened out for her. I questioned her about positions in the CIA. She said she was a loan officer and there were always people coming and going there, and that I should apply. (I had just been talking to an older lady downstairs at the Hecht Co. who was retiring and she said she was going to be receiving $86.00 each month, or something ridiculous like that, in retirement income, and she had been there many years.) So, despite the satisfaction of my work, I began to think. Plus the fact that several other girls had already left, or were leaving, for the CIA.

One girl whom I knew, and who had already left to go to the CIA, came in to visit me one day. She was very positive and even offered to drive me to Roslyn to fill out the application and take the tests. I took her up on the offer and about ten days later she picked me up and took me to fill out the forms and take the tests. There was not only a math, word meanings, and figurine test (where you pick out the one that is different) but there was also a six-page booklet of psychological questions. The application [security clearance] I was given to take home. There wasn't any way you could fill it out there. It called for everything you have ever done in your whole life, every place you have ever been in your whole life, and every person you have ever associated with in your whole life, plus a list of all relatives living out of the country! Oh, yes, and every ailment you have ever had in your whole life.

Well, it took me a week or so to fill that out. Then I sent it in. I can't remember the order in which they came, but I think the [granting of the] Security Clearance came next. Then the Polygraph, and then the physical (or vice versa). The interview fit in there somewhere too.

I had put down Credit Union as my first choice, Travel as my second, and Insurance third. I was interviewed by the Credit Union and told I could have a job as a "teller" but they thought I was over-qualified.

It was while all these obstacles were being "processed" that another girl in the Hecht Co. office came over and confided in me that she was going to work at the CIA. She said she was taking her polygraph the next week.

The next week finally came, and the following day she came in to me and said, "Pearl, I didn't get the job. Pearl, it was terrible. It was awful. They bombarded me with questions for almost three hours until finally I broke down and cried and told them they could stick the job up their ass—and I left."

Well, guess what? That was not to be the end of that story. About three weeks later, she came into my office again and said, "You are never going to believe this, Pearl, but I received a letter yesterday. I have been accepted for a position at the CIA!!"

Well, I knew the polygraph wasn't going to be pleasant. But finally my day of reckoning came. I was a nervous wreck when I arrived at the CIA Headquarters Building in McLean, VA, because I drove myself. I wasn't familiar with the area, and I had trouble finding a place to park. I finally had to ask someone.

Once inside the huge building I was directed to a room off to one side where I was to sign in and state my purpose for being there. The Polygraph office was then notified, and I was given an ESCORT BADGE to wear so that everyone seeing me would know that I was NOT one of them. A short while later my Escort arrived and I was taken to the Polygraph office.

After a short wait I was taken in and put into a chair that I can only describe now similar to an "electric chair". Then wires were attached to my fingers and I can't remember now where else! And then the barrage of questioning started. - Have you ever lied? Have you ever stolen anything? Have you ever taken drugs? Have you ever slept with another woman? Do you know any foreign nationals? . . . . and on and on and on.

When he asked me if I had ever stolen anything, I explained to him that I had taken a couple items from Lost and Found at the Hecht Co. that were going into the crusher. (I will never forget the day I saw Security throw a diamond ring and a bracelet [with a lot of foreign coins attached] into the crusher.) I said to him, "Ask me if I have ever stolen anything from the Hecht Co." He didn't like that. He said, "I'll ask the questions!"

Finally, after about two hours, he told me that I showed stress when he mentioned "drugs" and "falsifying my application". I said, "Drugs??? There isn't anybody more anti-drug than I am, and as for falsifying the application, there isn't anything on there that can't be checked out." He said, "Well, you might have left something off!!" I said, "Well, do you have the application there? Let me look it over. Maybe I forgot to put down that I have a hiatal hernia." He said, "No," he didn't have the application there. Then he excused himself and left the room.

Well - once he left the room a big grin came on my face. (I thought the whole thing was funny.) I had to put my hands on both cheeks to keep from laughing. I had to get that smirk off my face before he came back! ! (I learned later that they go outside and peek through a one-way mirror where they can see you, but you can't see them!)

Finally he came back. After a few more questions, it was determined that I had taken amphetamines ten or fifteen years before, but before I asked the Doctor for the prescription, I had accepted "ONE" of those pills from a neighbor friend—and that was considered an ILLEGAL DRUG!!!

He asked me if I had any left. I said, "Yes." He said, "How many?" I said, "Three." He said, "What are you saving them for?" I said, "Well, that was the only time I ever had control of my kids and the house at the same time in my whole life, so I am saving them in case I'm having company some time and want to get the house clean."

Shortly after that he told me I could go. As I was walking out the door, I turned around and said, "Did I pass?" He said, "Yes."

That was the beginning of my fourteen-year career at the Northwest Federal Credit Union. I started in as a teller. Then I became Assistant Head Teller, Loan Officer, Senior Loan Officer, Head Loan Officer, and finally, Credit Manager. It was a very rewarding and interesting place to work. I made many friends, and enjoyed the work.

A lot happened those twenty years we lived in McLean. The three older boys all graduated from college and all three went on to get their Master's Degrees. The two younger children became victims of the times. Their grades suffered and we transferred Wayne to Glebe Acres Prep School where he got his High School Diploma.

We transferred Craig from Langley High School to McLean High School where he got his High School Diploma.

I could tell some tales out of school here but I wouldn't want to get anybody in trouble. Some of their friends came from very influential families. Besides, one of the boys might want to write his own book someday.

I will tell you this one story, however. I was in the kitchen working one day when Howard came to the front door and said, "Pearl, come out here." I went out, and, lo and behold, there, right beside the garage, and in front of the house for all the world to see, was this huge five or six foot marijuana tree growing. Well, we were mortified. Neither one of us could understand why we had never noticed it before. We both had security clearances and we both could have lost our jobs. And Lord knows what else might have happened to us. Well, Howard pulled it out as fast as he could and dumped it over in the woods.

Wayne's Graduation picture. Can you find Wayne?

I remember one time when Craig asked to use the car to go to a New Year's Eve Party. I said, "Yes, but only if you promise to be home by 1 o'clock in the morning." So he promised!! Well, that night I woke up about 2 AM and went downstairs to check to see if he and the car were home. They were not! I stood in the window and paced the floor for a good hour. Then I woke Howard and got him all upset. Well, we stayed downstairs until about 4:30 grumbling and groaning, and worn out.

[Wayne is the third student from the left, back row.]

Finally we decided to go back to bed. I was so upset by that time that I said to Howard, "If the police call now I'm going to tell them, "You can keep him." Then we went to bed and went to sleep. - He came home at six o'clock in the morning.

It was during this time frame that we decided we needed a new couch in our family room. The one we had looked pretty shabby. So we went out and bought a new couch. I was on the phone calling "Goodwill" to pick up the old one when

Wayne came in. He said, "Don't give that couch away. I want it." I said, "You!!? What are you going to do with it?" He said, "I don't know, but it's too good to give away. One of my friends might want it." So we ended up putting it in the garage. About a year later I had to "BUY" the couch back from Wayne for $25.00 in order to get rid of it. Then we had to pay to have it picked up and taken away. (I can hardly believe some of the things we did now.)

Meanwhile Craig was out smashing cars. He had a total of six wrecks! One of our cars we had just finished paying $3,000.00 for to get it repaired because of an accident he had had. That very same day that the repairs were completed, Craig took the car and, this time, completely totaled it (putting part of McLean in total darkness because he had hit a telephone pole!).

Two of the accidents supposedly were not his fault. He was fortunate enough, and lucky enough each time, to have police witnesses. The two trucks which he totaled belonged to him. - Also the motorcycle which he damaged.

Needless to say we got into trouble with our insurance company. They raised our rates, and then they wanted to cancel. They finally agreed to keep us, if we would sign a paper stating that Craig would not be allowed to drive any of our cars at any time. (It was at this time that my poor mother was dying of cancer on Cape Cod. I will always feel bad that I was unable to go up and help out.)

Wayne in Army

Craig HS Grad

Sometime after Craig graduated from High School, he moved out of the house. At that time we allowed Wayne to take over one of the upstairs bedrooms. I expected him to sleep there and keep the room neat. He was told he could not put any nails in the wall.

Well, we came home one day and found he had flags tacked all over the walls. Gradually an ice box was moved in with banners pasted all over it, and then came a fish tank—with two piranha and some half eaten gold fish swimming around!! Sometime later the piranha developed a fungus around their mouths, thank goodness! One day we came home and found them out on the lawn - dead.

Wayne was still going through the rebellious stage at the time of his graduation from Glebe Acres. The night of the graduation Howard and I went with our goodies for the reception afterwards, and a gift for Mrs. Crigler, the School Headmistress. Wayne stood outside and peeked in the windows, refusing to come inside for his own Graduation!

Fortunately for us, that phase of their lives and our lives finally came to an end. (They were the longest years of my life.) Wayne turned very anti-drug after that. And went into the Army. Craig had settled into an apartment in Falls Church with another fellow—and he had a girlfriend.

Some months later, after Wayne had gone into the Army, Craig decided to move back home. We told him he could have the lower level. What we didn't know was that a pregnant girlfriend was moving in with him!! (No offense to you Mandy. We are happy that you did.) The three of them, Craig, Mandy and our precious granddaughter, Christina, stayed for almost three years, until we helped them buy a house on Ware Road in Falls Church.

Howard with Christina when she was living at our house.

A year after they moved into their new house they had another baby – precious Michael. Three years later they were married. We had the wedding at our house on Box Elder Court on 11 December 1990, with only family relatives invited. Thanks to Kevin and Linda the decorations were striking. They had streamers from the chandelier and balloons all over the dining and living room ceilings. The dining room table held the wedding cake as the centerpiece with live fir boughs around it. The rest of the table held the refreshments for the reception. The wedding itself was really cute. It took place underneath the archway between the dining room and living room with the relatives sitting and standing in the living room.

A Justice of the Peace came to the house to perform the ceremony. The wedding march was played from a tape and Mandy came down the three steps from our upper level on the arm of her father, who was dressed in one of those German colorful tuxedos. They were preceded through the living room to the archway by first, Killer (their dog), and then Christina and Michael, the flower girl and ring bearer. It was really a cute wedding.

Afterwards we all had dinner, meats and several salads and staples, with the wedding cake for dessert. Right after the wedding, and before the meal, we all had champagne in tiny plastic champagne glasses decorated with hanging streamers by Kevin and Linda. Kevin gave the "toast".

The one incident I forgot to tell you about which made a profound change in my way of thinking about religion was the birth of our precious little granddaughter. We had all sons, so we were thrilled to have a little granddaughter! When she was probably around two months old, Howard began to talk about having her baptized. I began to think, too, that his was a good time for me to start back to church. Once the kids had all left home, Howard had been going to church every Sunday and every Holy Day, all by himself! I was beginning to feel guilty. Howard had always been a good husband, and a good father.

Why, I could remember that from the time all of our boys were about three months old, when he was home at night, he would take them in the shower with him, with a visor around their heads so the soap wouldn't get in their eyes when he washed their heads. He'd soap them all down and rinse them all off and hand them out to me to dry and dress for bed. The kids loved it. When they got a little older he got into the tub with them. I can remember one time seeing him in the tub with the two younger ones. They were cleaning out his belly button and between his toes with a toothbrush! - And many a time I saw him sitting on the edge of the bathtub shaving, with the little ones faces all lathered up trying to shave, too, with shavers that didn't have any blades. He really tended to those kids as much as I did.

Now, to get back on track. Howard went to two different Priests in McLean to try to get Christina baptized. He was turned down by first one, and then the other, because Christina's mother and father were not members of the church. They told him to do it himself!! (What Howard didn't know was that I had baptized Christina the day after she was brought home from the hospital. When I told him he confided that he, too, had also baptized her that same week!) To this day I will never understand why they could not baptize that innocent child. If they didn't want to do it in the church, they could have at least offered to come to the house to do it—not do it yourself!!

That was the time they lost me. That was when I began to think about churches in general. They have all become businesses! Gone are the old days when I was taught God is good, God is love!! Today the churches all want power to force their beliefs on everybody else. I always thought there was supposed to be a separation between church and state. I believe in God. My God is a good God. I also believe that mistakes are made here on earth. And I also believe that God gave us each a brain and expects us to use it to correct those mistakes. I am very sure that God did not intend earth to become a torture chamber, which is what it is now for some people.

There are some issues that should not be decided by government nor dictated by any group of people. I will never understand why Pat Buchanan, who has NO children at all, should be the one to dictate, or make the decision that others should have babies. Neither do I believe that I should be the one to decide that my neighbor has to have another baby. Or vice versa. How do we get out of this rut this world is in? How do we get back to MYOB?

I have advised all of my children not to have any more children. (But the ones who can have children aren't listening to me.) This world is mixed up. This world is rotten. Even politics is rotten today. That $20 million spent digging up dirt on President Clinton fourteen years ago (Whitewater), even if he is guilty of something, isn't going to help the country one bit. That money could have been put to much better use. Shame on you D'Amato.

As for Paula Jones, who claims President Clinton made a pass at her. - So what??? I'll bet there isn't a girl in the world today over twenty who hasn't been propositioned some time in her life. I always thought that was the name of the game in life! She should have been flattered that somebody of that stature paid any attention to her at all. He didn't rape her. - And he didn't become a nuisance.

So now you can see that I am a bitter old lady. But not really. Only when I think of some of these worldwide issues. Basically I am a happy person. - Thanks to Howard.

Editor's Note: And Mom had no idea this was awaiting us!

I must say that he may not have been the easiest person to live with all my life. but he certainly has been a fun person to live with all these years. He truly is funny at times. Last week a good friend of mine called up. I was in the bathroom. Howard answered the phone. She said, "What are you people doing?" He said, "Well, we were just having an argument." She said, "Do you need a referee?" I heard him say "No, I think I've been knocked out!!"

Then the other night we called Bruce (Feb. 2nd) to wish him a happy birthday. We each got on a phone. They were not home so the answering machine came on. Simultaneously we said, "Happy Birthday, Bruce." Then Howard said, "I suppose you are out to dinner with Kevin and Linda" (they went out to ski and visit for a week). I said, "Well, I hope you are all having a good time." Then Howard said, "We are getting ready to go to bed right now." And I said, "So don't call back!" Then we signed off.

About seven or eight minutes later our phone rang. Howard picked it up first and I heard him say, "Hello, you have reached the Williams residence. We cannot come to the phone right now, but if you will leave your name and number at the sound of the beep, we will get back to you as soon as we can. - Then he W-H-I-S-T:L-E-D. I picked up in the middle of it and I could hear Kevin laughing to kill himself. – It really was funny.

Oh yes, I forgot to tell you about David's wedding. That was another big event in our lives. David was married to Jennifer Clarkson in Lambertville, New Jersey, on 12 May 1990. A couple weeks before the wedding when I was talking to David, I told him that we would drive to his house on the way to the wedding and I would ride with him to Lambertville. Some days later I was talking to Kevin and he told me that Joey Syiek was having a bachelor party for David the night before the Rehearsal Dinner and they would all be staying at Joey's overnight. I said to Kevin, "Oh, then David will go from there directly to the wedding." (Joey's place was so much closer to Lambertville than David's.) Kevin said, "Yes."

Well, the day before the wedding we started out with Craig, Mandy, Christina, and Michael in our car! Craig insisted on driving because he thought his arm, which had a huge cast on it, would be more comfortable on the driver's side. Two or three weeks before he had gone to a bar with another friend for a couple beers. When they left he was mistaken for another fellow who had had a fight in the bar earlier in the evening. The one who came out the worst had gone home and picked up a Samurai sword to finish that fellow off! Craig was the mistaken recipient of this fellow's anger and received a slice halfway through his hand because of it. A gruesome injury, the surgeon had to reattach the ring finger and the little finger. [The story that I heard about those injuries was a tad different. There *was* a bar and a *Samurai sword*, but there was also a *high speed car chase from the bar* with Craig the pursuer. We felt the fellow (who would do prison time for this assault) only meant to scare Craig off with a partial swing. But when Craig lifted his left arm to defend himself, the guy couldn't stop the sword in time.]

Well, the first thing to happen on the trip was that we were following a big sand truck bouncing down the highway and losing debris out the back. Howard told Craig to slow down and get away from the truck. But Craig is not that quick to take orders! By the time he did slow down a stone from the truck had bounced down the road smack into our car cracking the windshield! Howard saw the whole thing as if it were happening in slow motion: bounce, bounce, bounce, crack.

Next came me. I almost choked to death in the back seat on a piece of chicken. We had stopped earlier at a fast food chicken place. We still had some left over in a box. Mandy and I were sneaking a piece in the back seat when a piece of mine slipped down my throat and my throat completely closed around it. I couldn't breathe and didn't know what to do, so I took both hands and slapped Craig on the back of his head as hard as I could with my left hand and I slapped Howard on the back of his head with my right hand. They both turned around and I started making funny noises and pointing to my throat. With that Mandy started pounding me on the back as hard as she could. Craig had to cross over one lane to get to the side of the road. Howard and Craig both jumped out. It wasn't until they started pulling me out with both hands that the chicken dislodged and I was able to breathe again. Craig was so upset that he took the rest of the chicken and threw it into the field on the side of the road. (Later we wished we had it because Christina was hungry.)

After that I got very silly thinking about it in the back seat. I thought, what if I had died? Can you imagine pulling up to a wedding and the other kids asking, "Where's Mom?" "Oh, she died on the way. She choked on a piece of chicken!!"

I must say though that I did feel funny going by that Marcus Hook Road leading to David's house. I wish I had given it a little bit more thought. After the bachelor party David had gone home the next morning so that he would be there to meet us. (We didn't go there because we thought he was going directly from Joey's to the wedding!) We arrived at the Lambertville Inn, expecting to find David there. We waited and watched, and wondered why he wasn't there. Craig was down in the office when the phone call came wanting to know if we were there. The man turned the phone over to Craig. David said, "What in hell are you doing there?" and he hung up on him.

After that we were all upset. It seemed like ages before David got there. I was so happy to see him. He only had about twenty minutes left to pick up all of the tuxedos before the rental place closed!!

Poor David said he was sure upset. He said he had called the hospital and the State Police to see if there had been any accidents. But after that we all calmed down. The tuxedos got picked up and we all went to the Rehearsal Dinner at the Yellow Brick Toad Inn, and had a great time.

The next day was the wedding. It was a very nice wedding, but poor Howard had to read a portion of the Bible with his bifocal sunglasses. The day before we left home he couldn't find his glasses anywhere. We all looked and looked. That afternoon Jim Reedy came by. He had been doing some work for us. We happened to mention the glasses to him. When he was leaving he noticed something in the street out by the mailbox. And, sure enough, there were Howard's glasses all smashed to smithereens. There wasn't a piece of glass left in them and the frames were one mangled mess. (Howard had taken the trash out to the street that morning to be picked up by the trash truck, and they must have fallen out of his pocket then. Then the mailman must have come along and run over them!)

After the service Howard managed to leave the sunglasses in the tuxedo and they were taken away to the Clarkson home, about twenty miles away, to be returned to the rental agency!! So we had to trounce down there to get them. - And Kevin lost a good pair of 14K cuff links.

But next comes the funniest part of the wedding of all! After the wedding and reception, David and Jennifer returned to her parents' house to pick up her things and change before leaving on their honeymoon to Barbados. David said to Jennifer,

"Where is your suitcase?" Jennifer said. "At the foot of the stairs." So David went to the foot of the stairs and there were three suitcases. He said, he thought to himself, Boy, Jennifer is sure taking a lot of clothes! ! But he didn't say anything. So they got in the car and drove off. Now the Clarkson's had two guests that evening who had flown in for the wedding. One was from California and I don't know where the other one was from [Wimbledon, England]. Their suitcases had disappeared!!

When David and Jennifer reached the Hilton Hotel in Philadelphia where they were spending the night before leaving for Barbados the next morning, David opened the trunk and said to Jennifer, "Why did you bring so many clothes?" She said, "Me? They are all your suitcases!" David said, "No, they're not. They are yours!" When they got inside the hotel, there was an urgent message for Jennifer to call home!! Jennifer's brother, Ken, had to go to Philadelphia the next day to retrieve the suitcases and return them to their rightful owners. (David and Jennifer called us from Barbados a few days later to tell us about that luggage caper.)

My Philosophies!

Now for My Philosophies!

During my later years at the CIA I became an outspoken critic of many of our everyday problems in life. (Nothing to do with the CIA.) When anybody said something I didn't agree with I wasn't afraid to speak up. (I was usually all by myself though, speaking up!)

On Gays: I don't think they should be condemned. I think they should be treated as equals and given the SAME privileges as everybody else. God didn't make us all alike. He gave us all different tastes, looks, and beliefs. Who are we to say that they have to believe the same as us!!

I worked with a bunch of gays at the Hecht Co. I know they were gay because one of my friends, the Interior Decorator, who was not gay, was invited to one of their parties. They were the most hard working, polite and pleasant individuals I have ever worked with.

On Capital Punishment: Yes, I do believe in capital punishment. But not as it is today. I believe that any individual when it had been determined that he or she is unrehabilitatable, or is unsafe to be put out into society again, or should not be allowed out into society again, as punishment, should be put to death. - Not as a revenge (You can't bring dead people back), but for the betterment of the world. They should be given sodium pentothal (like they do when you have an operation) and put to sleep mercifully. Not the sadistic methods they have today - electric chair, gas, hanging and shooting.

Even the lethal injection they give today is sadistic. I read in the paper once that after the lethal injection blood runs out their nose and mouth. To me that isn't necessary. All they need to do is stop the heart. After all, these criminals have sick brains and they do have mothers and relatives, you know.

It has already been proven that all of these barbaric methods do not deter crime. Just remember it's the warped and sick brains causing them.

On Drugs: I would like to see this country legalize drugs. It would put all drug dealers out of business. Many of the other crimes such as break-ins, little old ladies being bopped on the head, bank robberies, murders, - all kinds of crimes - would be cut way back so that the streets would be safe to walk on again.

My Philosophies!

They should start with a massive educational program. This subject needs a lot more thought and study put into it. But, certainly something needs to be done about it along those lines.

On Churches: I think they have now become businesses and should be taxed.

On Medicare and Euthanasia: Here, once again, is the consequence of NOT having freedom of religion. We should be able to go into every nursing home in this country and put to sleep every individual (on Medicare or otherwise) who is old and beyond help, and who is a burden to themselves. - UNLESS THE INDIVIDUAL REQUESTS OTHERWISE. If the individual is incapable of making a decision, then the burden should fall upon their families.

Once again, I will reiterate, I do believe in God. If God is trying to take a life here on earth, why not help him out? Has anybody ever given that a thought? Medicare problems can only get worse as long as we prolong the dying process and let so many doctors get away with fraud. I see no hope for the burdens of our young people in the future proceeding as we are today.

A month or so ago the St. Petersburg Times, a great newspaper, ran a full page article on "Death with Dignity" by Lucy Morgan, with letters from the public. I was appalled and frustrated by the antics of some of our medical profession.

One woman wrote in that a Psychiatrist was called in for her comatose mother. He charged $80.00 per visit and visited each day she was in the hospital!! When the St. Petersburg Times called this Doctor to find out who authorized the visits, he refused to tell them! Now, I ask you, why wasn't this Doctor made to return that money to Medicare?

Another lady wrote in about her elderly dying mother who had advanced to the wheel chair stage. While being given therapy to help her walk, she fell down and broke her hip! How ridiculous! This woman was dying of old age.

About the same time there was an article in the paper about a "sick beached whale" that was given a lethal injection so death would be "as humane as possible."

A few days later in the same paper was a letter from someone in St. Petersburg stating that she (or he?) guessed the whale was not covered by Medicare or else they would have "continued to force feed it and give it swimming lessons."

All of this money spent unnecessarily to keep people "already dead?" alive could be put to good use helping poor sick people who have no insurance.

I know of one girl who innocently overdosed on a substitute sugar sweetener. She didn't know it was harmful at the time. She was a heavy girl and she used the sweetener generously. She started getting headaches, but because she didn't have any insurance, she didn't go to the Doctor until she lost her eyesight. Today she is legally blind. She is in her early 30's and has one child.

One more story I should tell you about which appeared in the same article in the St. Petersburg Times. One family got fed up with all the tests being performed on their poor mother in the hospital so they decided to take her home to die. When they went to pick her up to take her home, they asked the Doctor if he would give her a little morphine; enough to keep her comfortable for the ride home. They were turned down because, Heaven forbid, that was an addictive drug!! Well, they put her in the car and drove home. Every little bump they would go over she would moan and groan. After they got home they were reading her medical record - and discovered that she had 26 broken bones in her spine!! She died the next morning.

I SAY: All the more power to you Dr. Kevorkian, AND Wake up America before it's too late.

And now for the Justice System, last but not least! I think that our Justice System, although it may be one of the best in the world, still leaves a lot to be desired. After watching the O.J. Simpson trial, I know there was many a day when I had high blood pressure. Our system bends over backwards to protect the criminal and doesn't do enough to obtain justice for the victims.

For one thing in this country, everyone is innocent until proven guilty. I think in some instances, some people should have to prove their innocence. In the O.J. Simpson case, with all that evidence against him, he should have had to answer many questions. But, No, he was allowed to sit back, smug as a rug, and say NOTHING, leaving a lot of questions unanswered. His answers would have meant more to me than anything anybody else had to say. It is WRONG, and a poor law, for him not to have taken the stand.

Another thing that bothers me is the outrageous amount of money being awarded in law suits. Take the case of Rodney King, who was beaten unmercifully by several police officers. Now I think Mr. King should have been reimbursed for all of his expenses plus maybe $200,000.00 for pain and suffering. But $3.5 million? Come on. He was the one who caused the whole thing in the beginning - which culminated in two police officers losing their jobs and going to prison. Now, I am not defending the police officers. I think they got what they deserved. From what I have seen there are probably a good number of bullies on the police force. But to reward Mr. King with three and a half million dollars, plus the expenses of his attorneys in addition? Outrageous.

It is things such as this that have caused me to become so frustrated sometimes. It just makes me wonder, where is the common sense in this world?

My Retirement Years

Now to get on with my story. Here we are, old and gray, and retired. Howard retired on September 30, 1991, and I retired on October 31, 1991.

The past four years since we retired have been busy years. The summer before we retired we purchased a quaint rundown ranch home at 17 Milne Road in Osterville, the town where I grew up. It is less than 1/2 mile from the old homestead and Howard's old home.

Our retirement home in Osterville

It was nice being back with our relatives and being able to recognize and say "hello" to old acquaintances again. We had been gone for 40 years. It was interesting, and now I know how Rip Van Winkle felt! All of the faces had aged and a new generation or two had popped up. It was fun trying to figure out who belonged to whom.

And I was amazed at how many people couldn't recognize me. I gained over 80 lbs. over the years. Even my old good friend Priscilla Wittenmeyer didn't know who I was!! But I had trouble figuring out who she was, too.

Well, the first couple years on the Cape we were not at a loss for things to do. The house required a lot of repairs. We had a new roof put on the house, garage, potting shed and stable, a new dining room floor laid, cement poured in both the unfinished portion of the basement and in the stable. Extensive electrical work was done and an all new kitchen put in, including cabinets, not to mention all the painting that was done inside and out. An outside shower was installed, and the garage, potting shed and stable shingled. This past year a whole new heating system was put in. Howard took on the project of removing and leveling the back field which resulted in an injury to his arm that required an operation at Lahey clinic in Boston.

Our property is almost one full acre. He not only has a garden each year with tomatoes, cucumbers and peppers, but he also has a couple apple trees and a grape arbor! Between his garden, golf, and Wayne, who also moved to the Cape, Howard really lives a full life while we are on the cape.

Now I must not forget to tell you about the squirrel incident. we had been in our Osterville home less than a year. Howard's sister-in-law, Barbara, was visiting from New Mexico. We had invited her sister, Eleanor, and her niece, Marilyn Lawrence, from Concord, down for the day. They had no sooner arrived and were in the yard no longer than two minutes, when Howard was attacked by a squirrel! We were standing in a circle greeting each other by the car, when all of a sudden, Howard started to dance! We all looked down and here was this squirrel wrapped around his leg. (He had on shorts.)

As he was trying to get it off, it bit him a couple times. Then it ran up the tree a few feet, turned around and looked at us, and then came back down and jumped on Marilyn, running up her back and down her arm where it bit her as she was trying to get it off. Then it ran up the tree again. When it was six or eight feet off the ground, it turned around once again—this time looking at Eleanor. Then he (or she) came down again and jumped on Eleanor. It ran up her back, under her sweater, and came out at her neck and sat on top of her head—she put her hand up to try to get it off and that was when she got bitten! She got the worst bite of all. It went through to the bone on her finger! Marilyn was the one who finally got it off her mother. Then it ran up the tree a few feet and turned around once again. This time looking at me! (we were all in a trance.)

Howard was the one to come to his senses first. He hollered, "Run in the house, Pearl. So Barbara, Eleanor and I all ran towards the house, with the squirrel following right behind us! As we closed the screen door, we could see the squirrel coming up the bulkhead where he leaned over, stood up, and tried to see in.

Then it turned around and went out in the yard again where Howard grabbed a kiddie swimming pool we had out there, and tried to catch it. (We were all sure it would have to be tested!) He thought he had it trapped under the pool, but as he cautiously walked up to it, the squirrel came from the back of the pool, jumped on top, and very defiantly looked at him! With that Howard ran to the garage to get something so that he could hit it. The squirrel took off after him. After Marilyn yelled, "He's in there with you, Howard," Howard grabbed the first thing he could find, which wasn't heavy enough. They both came out of the garage together, and Howard did manage to hit it slightly, but then it ran away.

Meanwhile I was inside calling 911. Telling them to send the Police with a gun. By the time the police did arrive, the squirrel was long gone. The police wanted to call an ambulance, but we decided to go over to the hospital in our own car.

By the time we pulled up to the Emergency Entrance, Eleanor was feeling faint and nauseous. We had to get a wheelchair to take her in. (Of course we all thought the squirrel had already given her something!)

CAPE & ISLANDS

CAPE COD TIMES
TUESDAY, SEPTEMBER 15,
1992

Nutty squirrel puts the bite on Osterville host, guests

By TRISHA CURRIER FLANAGAN
STAFF WRITER

OSTERVILLE — "All I could think of was in Caddyshack, where Bill Murray was chasing that gopher," said Howard Williams, using a movie scene to describe the melee that broke out in his Osterville yard when a squirrel attacked a group of people.

Williams, of 77 Milne St., and two guests were treated at Cape Cod Hospital, Hyannis, for multiple bites inflicted by the pugnacious rodent.

Williams, his wife, Pearl, and sister-in-law Barbara Williams, were in the yard at noon Sunday greeting their arriving guests, Marilyn Lawrence and her mother Evelyn Lawrence, both of West Concord.

"All of a sudden I felt something on my leg and I screeched. It was a squirrel, and he wrapped his legs around my left calf and bit me a couple of times," Williams said.

He threw the squirrel onto the ground, and the animal jumped onto Marilyn Lawrence, climbed up her leg and bit her on the upper arm. She threw it off, and it ran to a tree, climbing halfway up.

"It looked at us, then it came back down and attacked Marilyn's mother. It ran up her leg, under her sweater, and out at her shoulder. It grabbed her by the top of the head," Williams said. Mrs. Lawrence, 83, managed to swipe the animal off.

Pearl and Barbara Williams and Evelyn Lawrence ran into the house, the squirrel chasing them. Then it turned and headed toward Howard Williams and Marilyn Lawrence, who continued to stand on the lawn, too amazed to move.

They grabbed a small plastic wading pool and tossed it toward the squirrel, hoping to trap it underneath, but when they cautiously approached the pool, the squirrel jumped from behind it, over the overturned top, and defiantly stared at them.

"I ran into the garage to get something to hit him with. I got a 10-foot pole, and he came after me again. I hit him, and he came into the garage with me," Williams said. After a brief standoff, the animal ran away and Williams called the police department.

A Barnstable natural resources officer searched unsuccessfully for the combative creature.

Natural resources officer Doug Kalweit said the incident was "very unusual" and that the department has not received reports of other bellicose squirrels in the town's villages.

The incident has given the Williamses and the Lawrences a healthy respect for squirrels. Williams said he will be on the lookout in case the creature returns.

"We're going to keep our car windows closed all the time, to make sure he isn't in the car. And we're going to be very careful about squirrels," he said. "But you know, we did laugh a lot afterwards."

As it turned out, there really wasn't much to worry about. They put a bandage on her finger and she had to get a tetanus shot. We were told that squirrels do not carry rabies. Marilyn was told the same thing later by Natural Resources where she worked.

When we came out of the hospital, we were still all nerved up and none of us were hungry; so we decided to go to Mildred's Chowder House for "coffee", where the strangest thing happened! We all ordered big meals, ate like pigs, and laughed ourselves silly. Howard and I both said that nobody will ever come to visit us again, if that is the kind of reception they get!!

Now to get on with my "Retirement Years."

In 1988, when we were on vacation that year, we purchased a two-bedroom, two-bath condo at 650 Island Way (a short distance from our old home on Leeward Island) that we had every intention of spending our retirement winters in. Well, we had a good tenant who had been in the condo from the time of purchase. Being the old softies that we are, we hated to ask her to move, so we decided to find a place down here for us to rent for three months each winter until she decided to move out.

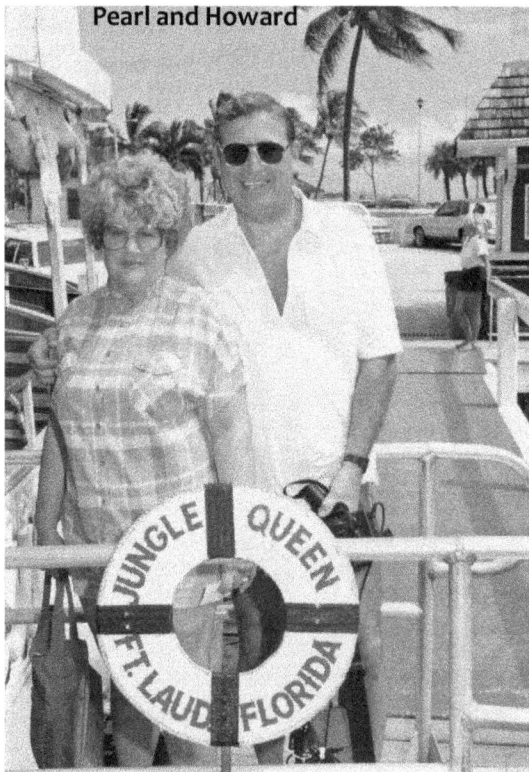

Pearl and Howard

While on vacation in March 1993 we began to look in New Port Richey near the Holiday Inn where we usually spent our vacations. Because the Realtor couldn't show us any rentals (they said they would have to send pictures!!) they showed us places that were for sale. (A smart move on their part.)

After taking us into several small condos that were not appealing to us, they finally brought us to see a three-bedroom two-bath rundown condo at the Sea Castle. It was very spacious and had a nice layout. Despite the fact there wasn't anything appealing to us inside we both saw the potential right away! It was on the 6th floor and the enclosed balcony on the back had a fantastic view - overlooking a marina, a very nice restaurant (Leverock's), the Holiday Inn where we stayed and a shopping center, plus a fantastic view of Rt. 19. It had an all-night deli which sells the cheapest gas in town right outside the door. The shopping center which we could walk to had not only a Publix, but an Eckerd Drug, Bank, Hallmark Store, Sally's Beauty Supply, Levitz, Jewelry Store, Beall's Clothing Store, Tax Collector, P. O. (at Beall's), Laundromat, Restaurant and several others.

That night after we returned to Holiday Inn, neither one of us could stop thinking about that fantastic view from the Sea Castle. The next morning Howard said, "I think we should buy it." I said, "Well, you know, if we got it all fixed up, when our tenant moves out, we could sell it. I'm sure we could always get our money out of it."

We must have been gluttons for punishment!! We had just finished two years of stress and frustration refurbishing our Osterville home, and now we were going to do the same thing in Florida!! We bought the condo the next week and closed in May 1993.

Now comes the tale of woe! The refrigerator compressor was gone so we could not use the refrigerator, the garbage disposal was disconnected under the sink so that all the water ran out on the floor, the same with the dishwasher, all the water came out on the floor. And last, but not least, was the shower off the Master bedroom. The first time Howard used it, it leaked into the Condo below. We had gone out to get something to eat and came home and found a note on our door, - DO NOT USE SHOWER - LEAKS ON CONDO BELOW. We knew about the refrigerator, dishwasher, and sink before we closed, so we were given a $700.00 allowance, but the shower was a complete surprise.

Needless to say, the next two seasons we had our work cut out for us. We re-carpeted, removed wallpaper, repainted, replaced everything in the kitchen including cabinets and floor, replaced shower in master bath and redecorated and repapered both bathrooms, including new sinks and counter tops, replaced hot water heater and bought all new furniture and window treatments. Now that it is over with, it is like having a baby: you forget about all the pain and frustration.

To top everything off, the tenant, whom we so gallantly protected, gave us notice and moved out of our Clearwater Condo eight months after we bought this one. (That was exactly two years ago.) But that was too late for us. We had already fallen in love with not only the Sea Castle Condo, but the area, conveniences, and people. To date the Clearwater Condo has not been sold. If it doesn't sell in another month or so, we will rent it.

Today we are very happy. We have the best of both worlds: a cute little Early American home on Milne Road in Osterville for the summers and an elegant condo in the warm Florida climate for the winters.

This winter is one of the best winters I have ever experienced in my whole life. The condo is completely finished and we have made some great friends not only in the Sea Castle but in the surrounding area. We were fortunate to have Mary and Vic Hudson move into the Sea Castle this year. We eat out often with them and Mary is my constant pool companion, along with Judy Baker.

Tonight we have been invited to Anna and Howard Ryder's for dinner. They have become very good friends. Let me tell you how we met them. In March 1994 we had flown to Cape Cod to take care of our Income Tax. When we went to the Hyannis Airport to fly to Boston to return to Florida, the weather was very bad, rainy and very windy. At first the flight was canceled, but then, about two minutes later, they announced the plane would fly. We all rushed on to the plane.

When we arrived in Boston we went to the area where our plane would take off for Florida. It was while we were sitting there that a complete stranger came over to us and said, "Do you have a son named Wayne?" I said, "Yes." He said, "Well, my name is Chester Ryder. When we took off in the plane at Hyannis I was in the air when I discovered I still had the car keys in my pocket!! My wife had brought me to the Hyannis Airport and I knew she had no way to get home. I called her just now, and she said a nice young fellow named Wayne Williams gave her a ride home to get her keys!"

Then Chester told us that he was going to New Port Richey also. I asked him how he was getting there from the Airport. He said his brother was picking him up. He also said they might have room for us. We didn't want to impose, so when the plane landed in Florida we went on about our business. It was while we were out checking on taxis and limos that we heard our name come over the pager. That's when we first met Anna and Howard. She even kissed me good-bye when I got out of the car. I felt as though I had just found a long lost sister!

That's one thing I can tell you about Florida, they have some super people living here.

All is not quite as rosy as it might sound however. Let me tell you a little bit about my health. About 18 years ago when I applied for employment at the CIA, it was discovered that I had diabetes. For about eight years it was controlled by pills. But then, about ten years ago, I had to start taking insulin. I know I never did put enough effort into controlling my weight and food intake. Neither have I put enough effort into exercising.

I am just not an exercise person and I just don't know how people can stay on diets. I am a fun person, and I like to eat. I always said I'd rather eat and die young than starve and live a miserable life. It's funny, but I still feel that way today. I have had good control of my blood sugar for a couple of years now. But not my weight. I take about 160 cc$_s$ of insulin daily. In three weeks I will be 69 years old and I weigh 200 lbs. exactly. (I know that sounds like a lot but I carry the weight well.)

I still have a good outlook on life and enjoy shopping, sunbathing and eating out, and socializing with my friends and family.

My eyes so far appear to be the only thing that have been damaged by the diabetes. Shortly after we retired to Osterville, I had two cataract operations. I have had three laser treatments since then for diabetic retinopathy. I have lost some of my vision but I am thankful I can still read. I love the daily newspapers, USA Today and St. Petersburg Times, Danielle Steel, V. C. Andrews, Mary Higgins Clark, and People Magazine. Also, the scandal sheets, National Enquirer and the Star, and the Cape Cod News.

This past winter I have been experiencing some numbness in my hands, if I sleep the wrong way, and some numbness on the tip of my tongue and around my mouth when I have a low blood sugar attack, which happens every once in a while. I am very faithful about taking my insulin and checking my blood. One time I took an overdose of insulin in the evening. It was by accident. I forgot I had already taken it. When it dawned on me what I had done, I got up every two hours all night and checked my blood. Each time it got down around 80, I would eat a few Cheese Nips. I know I should be eating glucose tablets, but they don't seem to work fast enough for me. Cheese Nips do.

My one other problem this winter is that my ankles and feet puff up every once in a while, especially after I have been on them any length of time. I do not use salt at all anymore and I buy salt-free bread and butter. Maybe now that I am experiencing a few problems, *that* will be the incentive to shed a few pounds!!

My greatest fear is that I will pre-decease my Howard and will not be around to take care of him when he gets old. Alzheimer's runs in his family. His grandmother, mother, and Uncle Carl all had it. I have already assured Howard that if he ever gets it and is unhappy and a burden to himself, I will see to it that he has death with dignity—carbon monoxide. If he doesn't want to get in the car for that purpose, I will give him a couple sleeping pills and take him for a ride around town until he falls asleep. (He has never told me NOT to do it.) By then I will be ready to go right along with him. I wouldn't want to live without him anyway.

Now that I have said my piece I want to assure you all that I am a happy stable person. I have every intention of living out my life to the fullest.

HERE LIES PEARL. LIFE FULFILLED

I am not depressed. I am very grateful for having lived such a wonderful life. As long as I can be beneficial to my family and friends, I want to stay alive. The day when I become unhappy and I am a burden to myself and to my family is the day I have every intention of connecting a hose to the back of the car and passing into oblivion.

I don't want anyone to feel sorry for me because I will have achieved my death with dignity.

To my family: I love you all. Please take care of each other.

Good bye World
and
Thank you God

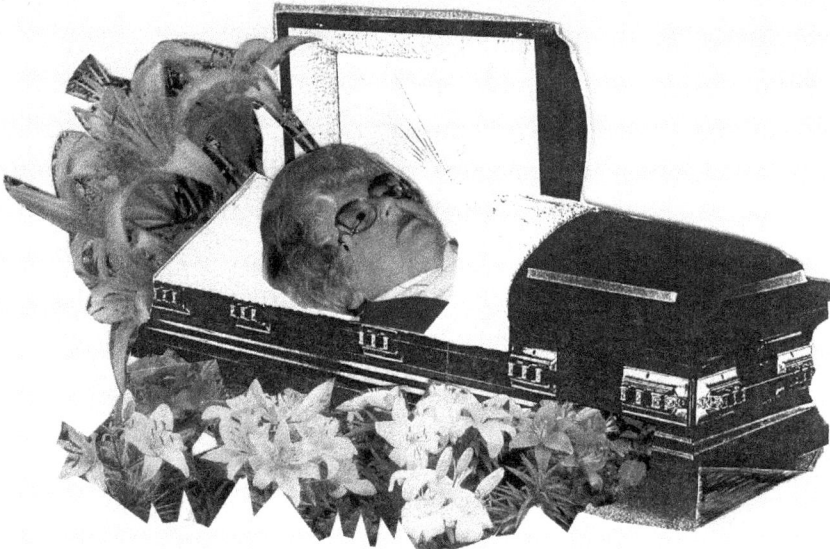

Families Are Forever

Families are Forever

Please keep us close together
And help us to be good
And always love each other
The way a family should.

When our lives are over
Please let us meet again
So we can be a family
Up in heaven, Lord.
Amen

—Author Unknown

Concluding Wish

Pearl would finish the first book on her adventures and philosophies in 1996, but she knew that she'd continue with a follow on book.

THE END

Now that this book is done
I must say, "It has been fun."
I know that all will not agree
with everything that I see.
And even though you may not hear it
This is "me" in my "free spirit".
They are my "treasures".
They bring me pleasures.
And if you think this has been YOUR
   "cup of stew",
Watch for my volume II

Pearl Williams
June 1997

Family of Pearl Marney Williams

February 1996

[Additional family members subsequent to 1996 in brackets]

FATHER: Fraser A. Marney
Born: 31 October 1896, Died: 06June 1956

MOTHER: Martha O. Marney
Born: 15 September 1902, Died: 05 September 1978

SIBLINGS Pauline (deceased), Osborne, Edison, Arthur, and Kenneth (deceased).

HUSBAND: Howard W. Williams, son of Francis A. and Louise Riedel Williams (both deceased), one brother, Paul (deceased).

CHILDREN:

Kevin, married to Linda Carter, no children.

Bruce, married to Christine Chambers, two children, Rebecca and Jonathan.

David, married to Jennifer Clarkson, one child, Spencer. [plus son Oliver]

Craig, married to Mandy Reiche, two children, Christina and Michael.

Wayne, unmarried. [Plus wife Bridget, biological daughter Dana Patrick, biological granddaughter Freya Halley]

Conclusion to The Adventures and Philosophies of an Old Lady

[Original Cover]

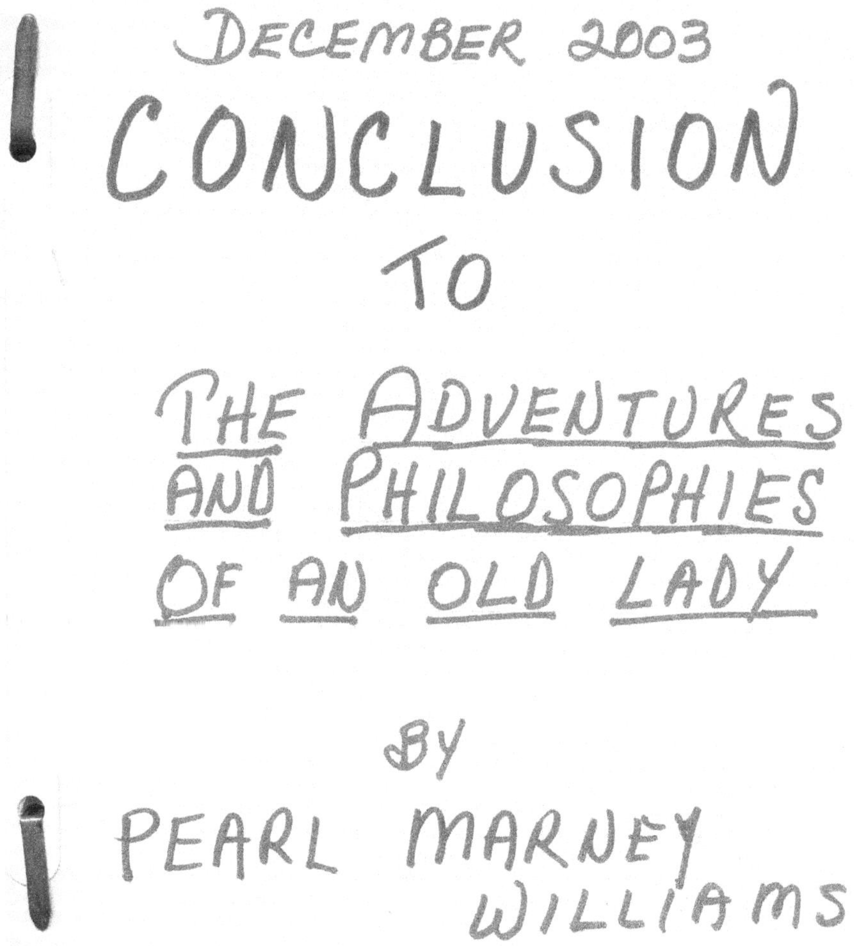

DECEMBER 2003

CONCLUSION

TO

THE ADVENTURES AND PHILOSOPHIES OF AN OLD LADY

BY

PEARL MARNEY WILLIAMS

The Golden Years that Tarnished

[This is book 2: the Conclusion to the Adventures and Philosophies of an Old Lady that Pearl completed in Dec 2003. In it she details continuing lifetime events with a heavy concentration on medical difficulties and end of life decisions. What she didn't know was that there would be many more events and she would live on until 2010.]

I fear my days are numbered here on earth and even though I didn't feel like writing at this time, my instinct tells me to get going. So, here goes…

It is now December 2003. In January 2002 I was diagnosed with Non-Hodgkin's lymphoma (a cancer that originates in your lymphatic system) with an inoperable tumor the size of a large orange at the stem of the colon. To start at the beginning, I had been extremely tired for some time. I remember one day while sun bathing at our Sea Castle condo in New Port Richey, FL saying to one of the girls, "Boy, I just feel as though it wouldn't take much to blow me away." My friend got very upset and said, "Pearl, don't say things like that. That is a terrible thing to say. Think positive!"

Well, it wasn't more than a few weeks later when I felt there was a balloon stuck in my waste in the right hand side! I noticed that I had to sit down a couple times when I was making our king size bed. I was having chills every afternoon and had to put heavy clothing on. I was blaming Howard for having the air conditioning down too low! Often I had to go to bed to get warm. I never thought to check my temperature. Plus I had a terrible itch on my back, backside, and ankles, which I rubbed with a stiff hair brush as hard as I could without taking the skin off! Many a night I had to jump up from sleep and run for the hairbrush! When it would start to burn, I would put Solarcaine on it.

Finally one day I noticed that I did have a fever. I told Howard that if the discomfort in my stomach didn't get better by morning I thought I should go to the Emergency Room. The next morning the balloon had spread to inside the front of my stomach, so I got up at 5 A.M., did the laundry and cleaned the house, and then we set out for the Emergency Room.

I was in the hospital from 15 December until Christmas Eve. I came home at 4:30 P.M. December 24th. They had determined after I was in there a short while that I had a bowel infection. Possibly C Diff, it was some kind of old people's disease that was contagious; so I was quarantined for a few days. I was put into a private room and everyone who came into the room had to wear a mask! However, with antibiotics, that was cleared up in short order: two or three days.

But during all the tests that they performed, a CT scan was done, and guess what—they had found a 7.4 cm mass in the upper part of my abdomen. They as much as told me that I had some kind of cancer, but they couldn't determine what kind! More tests would have to be run and biopsies taken!!

The holidays soon passed and next came the most miserable two years I have ever put in in my whole life! The beginning of many trips to the hospital. The first was for biopsies from the back of my neck and the lymph node under my right arm. Nothing showed up there so I was subjected to an exploratory operation—where I was cut down the center from the breast through the belly button to the pelvic bone. The tumor was found at the stem of the colon—but there wasn't anything they could do about it because it had too many blood vessels through it and they said they would have to take out all of my bowels and "you wouldn't want that!" So I was closed up again.

All of the sample biopsies they took turned out to be dead cells!! They said the tumor consisted of a white toothpaste type material enclosing a large number of blood vessels. My oncologist said that he knew that it was cancer, but they couldn't treat me until they found out for sure what kind it was.

In December I had had a mammogram done and they found three cysts under my right breast. Supposedly, they were benign. My primary care physician had referred me to a surgeon who assured me they were nothing to worry about!

Well, when all of the biopsies and the exploratory surgery proved fruitless, I was told by my oncologist that I was an "enigma." He said they were going to have to refer me to the Moffitt Cancer Center in Tampa. However, before he let me out of the office that day, he decided once again to check the cysts under the right breast. And, lo and behold, he determined that one of the cysts was attached to the skin. He immediately called the surgeon and ordered a biopsy.

So, once again, I was off to the hospital! All three cysts were removed—and—sure enough, the one attached to the skin proved positive for Non-Hodgkin's lymphoma. Now my doctor could treat me!

I had always said I would never take chemotherapy if I had cancer! And I had already told both my primary care physician and my oncologist that I wasn't having any chemo!! But, when I asked my oncologist how long I would last and he told me, "SIX MONTHS!!" I changed my mind and decided I would try it one time!! Then, of course, one time leads to another, and then another, to another, to another, until it is over with.

Next came my trip to the hospital to have a port put in. That was an experience in itself!! On 13 February 2002 I entered Community Hospital to have the intravenous port put into my chest for the chemo treatments. I entered the hospital at 7 A.M. and was taken to the O.R. around 10:30 A.M. Approximately 1 P.M. when I came to in the recovery room, a nurse was standing next to me and she said, "What is wrong with your heart." I said, "I don't know, but it is fluttering." She watched the monitor a while longer and then said, "It's all right. It's okay now." So I was taken to my room where I was released around 4 P.M.

After returning home, I felt funny but didn't know what it was. After dinner that evening, in the center of my chest it felt like a grub crawling around. Very strange!! That night when I went to bed, and turned on my left side, it felt like MORE THAN ONE GRUB crawling around—and it would take a bite out of me every once in a while. I got up at 12 midnight and sat on the couch for about two hours until I got tired enough to sleep again.

When I got up that morning I called the surgeon's office to find out if there was any way the port could have been put in wrong. I was assured that everything was all right; that I could expect a LITTLE discomfort a day or so after any operation. I said, "Well okay, if you say so."

The next day at 10 A.M. I had to go to Radiology Associates to get a MUGA scan, a nuclear medicine test to see if my heart muscles were strong enough to take the chemo. The *grubs* were still there. I was watching the monitor and saw that my heart was skipping a lot of beats. I said to the technician, "Is it normal to skip that many beats?" He said, "Has it done this before?" I said, "No, only since they put this port in." He said, "Have you ever been to a cardiologist?" I said, "No." He said, "Well, maybe you should—just for your own peace of mind."

After returning home from the test that day, I got very upset because of my heart skipping so many beats! And I still had the *bugs*. So I called the surgeon's office once again, explaining about the missing heart beats, in addition to the *bugs*!! This time the nurse phone operator went to the doctor for advice, and I was told the doctor wanted to look something up and he would call me back.

A couple minutes later they called and said my primary care physician had been notified and I would be contacted shortly to come in for an EKG. Two minutes later my primary care physician called and we went immediately to her office. She did a 10 second EKG where it only skipped one beat. But after hearing my story, she said she was putting me in the hospital overnight on a heart monitor. She said if everything was all right, I would be released in the morning.

We arrived at the ER at approximately 6:00 P.M. By 6:30, I was in a bed with a heart monitor on. By 8:30, there was a gurney outside my door waiting to take me up for chest X-rays!! This was done. That night I slept in a chair once again for comfort.

The next morning at 7:30 the doctor came in and said, "Mrs. Williams, we are going to have to pull your port. It has dropped down and migrated into the heart and is aggravating it." I said, "I knew something was wrong." He said, "I'm glad you told us. We have a very busy schedule today (which was a Saturday) but I will be done today, sometime this afternoon. Do not eat or drink anything." I assured him I would not.

That afternoon around 2:00, the gurney arrived to take me to the OR. When I came to in the recovery room, I knew right away I was back to normal. It made all the difference in the world. All the *bugs* and *biting* were gone. (They had cut two inches off the stem of the port.)

Next came the chemo treatments! These proved disastrous to my whole system. My body didn't like it one bit. After each of the first four treatments I ended up in the hospital for a week. I learned that chemo not only kills the bad cells but all of the good cells as well! Following each of my chemo treatments I took high doses of Prednisone each day for five days. I would feel fine until I stopped taking the Prednisone, but then all hell would break loose. Because the chemo had killed my immune system, the fevers would begin and I would be ordered into the hospital! I was treated for pneumonia, I was treated for infection, I was treated for thrombosis in the left leg and a large clot in the right leg, and I was treated for colitis in the blood stream. You name it, I had it!

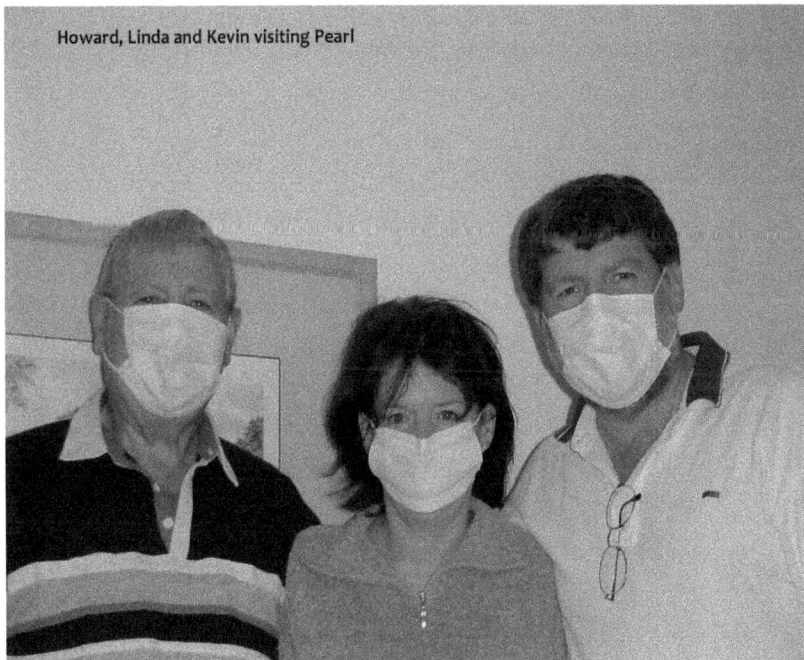

Howard, Linda and Kevin visiting Pearl

Kevin and Linda would help out when the folks were in Florida.

I had six different doctors working on me. I had not only my primary care and my oncologist, but an infectious disease specialist, a gastro-intestinal specialist, a cardiologist, and a urologist—in addition to a podiatrist and an eye doctor I had been seeing regularly for my diabetes. I went to the podiatrist originally because I thought I had gangrene in two toes! The nails turned completely black. He had to use a hot iron on one big toe and drill three holes in it to get the blood out. The other toe he tried to get the blood out, but it had been in there too long and had hardened!

Another time after a chemo treatment, I woke up one morning and looked in the mirror and almost fell over. The white in the right eye had turned completely black, with three psychedelic colors looking out at me: one red spot, one green spot and one yellow spot!!

I called the eye doctor right away and he took me in a couple hours later. A blood vessel had broken. The Doctor said that even though it looked really bad, there was no harm done and it should clear up in a few days. Which it did, thank goodness!

By the time the fifth chemo treatment came along (I had eight in all), they had come out with a new shot, called Neulasta, which supposedly had a tail on it and would take over when my white blood cell immune system got really low. That ended my trips to the hospital after the chemo treatments, but I still had to make two or three trips to the doctor's office each week for my blood to be checked. (I was getting a chemo treatment every three weeks.)

My blood was bad from day one. I had been being treated for anemia for about ten years, but no doctor ever suggested a CT scan! It wasn't until I changed doctors and went to my good Dr. Dina Jain that she said, "Why are you taking this Ferris Sulfate (iron)? There is something eating your red blood cells daily." She referred me to a hematologist.

My previous doctor kept taking more and more blood tests, thinking it was a mistake when my LDL always came back so high. (It was over 400, one of the signs of Lymphoma.) Never once did she refer me to a hematologist!

The previous doctor before her, when I complained about my collar bone and neck being all puffed up, sent me for X-rays. He went so far as to tell me that he had been sure I had cancer, but the X-rays showed it was a "fat" pocket, and nothing to worry about!! He also should have sent me for a CT scan or an MRI, but he did not.

I had made my appointment with the hematologist/oncologist, but it was before I could keep the appointment that I ended up in the hospital.

I will tell you here that at no time during my illness have I ever been depressed or down, DESPITE my ailment and discomfort—even when I asked the doctor how long I would last without treatment and the doctor replied, "6 months." It was as though he was talking about someone else!

Now, after my many, many trips to the hospital, I will give you a few tips about hospital care. I learned everything the hard way! The first is "LOOK OUT FOR YOURSELF." Try to stay as alert as you can and don't be afraid to ask questions. When I had my exploratory operation in January 2002, I was assured by my surgeon that I would be comfortable. I would be given morphine and be out of it for about three days! Well, when I did come to a day or so later, I found myself in the

Progressive Care Unit and was not in any pain whatsoever. However, I also found out that I was put into bed like a cement block!! I could move my head, arms, feet, and legs, but the rest of me would not budge.

I was warm so I pushed the blanket down and off my feet with my legs. Then I got very cold and was starting to get chills. There wasn't any way I could get hold of the blanket to pull it up. So I rang for the nurse. I could hear the bell ringing outside my door, but no nurse was coming. After about what seemed like a *very long* time the bell stopped! I thought, "Oh, good; she is on her way!" But no nurse came. By then I was getting very upset, so I rang the bell again. This time the bell went on — and off, immediately. So I pressed the alarm again.

A few minutes later the nurse came running in and said, "Mrs. Williams, you are not the only one in this hospital you know. We have to take care of emergencies first and we each have so many patients." I said, "How many patients do you have anyway, eighty-five?" She said, "No three—if you want private care you should have brought your own private nurse with you." I said, "Well, if I had known there was going to be no one here to care for me, I would have."

After that, I called my doctor and told her to get me out of there as "there is no one here to care for me!" She must have called the head nurse because I never did see that nurse again, and from there on they always responded in a short while.

And here is a tip for diabetics who take insulin! Never go to the hospital without something sweet, a candy bar or two in your purse. I had about three low blood sugar attacks during my many visits to the hospital—and they all happened in the middle of the night. Once when I was having one of those attacks in the wee hours of the morning, a nurse came in and caught me wiping my brow and eating a large chocolate almond candy bar. She said, "What is going on here?" I said, "I am having a low blood sugar attack!" She became very indignant and said, "You are supposed to call us when anything like that happens!" I took one good look at her and said, "You have got to be kidding. By the time you got here I would be dead!"

She immediately called for someone to come and take my blood sugar. It was 81—and I had already eaten half of that large chocolate bar. So it must have been pretty low. I could always tell when I was having a low blood sugar attack. I would get very warm. The sweat would start pouring off my head and my heart would start pounding like mad.

I learned very early on in my trips to the hospital that my body can't tolerate too much of that glucose IV fluid they fill you up with. My feet, body, and legs turn to wood. On about my fifth trip to the hospital, I noticed one evening that my legs were beginning to get hard, so I asked my nurse to please call my doctor to have it turned off. That was about 7 o'clock in the evening. About 10 o'clock that same evening the nurse came back. I asked her if she had called my doctor. She said, "No."

I thought, well it's too late in the evening now to call the doctor, and I was really upset to think that she didn't do it, so I said, "Well, I am ordering this infusion turned off; and if you don't do it, I will!" She said she would have to check with the head nurse. She came back and said the head nurse said that it could not be turned off because they had to keep the lines open for other medications, but they would turn the machine down from 65 to 15 or 20!! I checked after she left and she had turned it down to 30!! At least that satisfied me that it was better than it was before.

And, oh yes, the urologist. I must tell you about him. On one of my trips to the hospital I couldn't empty my bladder so they called in a urologist. They had already catheterized me twice and it hurt like the devil. It felt like a butcher knife being poked into me. I think they could hear me screech all over the hospital! And I do have a pair of healthy lungs!! (Or, I did have, I should say.) Well, anyway, the urologist said he would put in a catheter that would stay in place until they found out what the problem was. It was during this evening when he came in and he said it would be put in the next morning. I asked him if I could be put to sleep. He said, "No, it only hurts for a minute." I explained to him that it felt like a butcher knife going in. I told him I didn't understand, you can go to a dental office and they can give you laughing gas or something else to keep you comfortable. He said, they would give me a little sedation to calm my nerves! The next morning my primary care doctor came in early and I told her my predicament. She said she would order a morphine shot for me before the procedure was done.

After she left I thought, I have to find a way to urinate to get out of this mess. So I got out of bed and sat on the commode, turning every which way until finally , by some miracle, I was able to go. (And quite a bit, I might add.)

About an hour later the nurse came in with the syringe to give me the morphine shot. I said, "You can forget that needle. Look in the chamber. I was able to go." So she left—returning a short while later with the syringe. She said the head nurse said that I had to have it because it was ordered by the doctor!! I said, "Well, that's too bad. Go back and tell her that I refuse to have the shot or be catheterized." A couple hours later the urologist came in and I guess he didn't believe me, so he ordered a machine brought in to measure the urine in my bladder. (Such a simple little machine, on wheels, which came over the top of the bed about two inches above my stomach.) It was 1/8 full, so that was the end of that! And after that, I was always asked to go on my own.

Another funny experience, I had to go to Shands Cancer Hospital in Gainesville to swallow a camera to determine what was causing my internal bleeding. They put a very wide leather belt around my waste from which two good size boxes were hung. One on each hip with wires hanging down the front of me to my knees. (I felt like something from outer space.) After I swallowed the camera at 8:30 A.M., I was told I could leave and "go anywhere I wanted!!" But to return at 4 P.M. for them to remove the recorders. (Can you imagine "going anywhere you want" with all that paraphernalia on?!) We took the shuttle back to the hotel where we stayed until I passed the camera—at 1:20 P.M. that same day!

When they gave me the camera to swallow I told them everything I ate went right through me in short order. I asked if they had one of those plastic containers to put into the toilet to catch whatever came out so that I would not miss the camera. They said, "Oh, we don't have anything like that, but you don't have to worry, the camera won't come out for 24 hours!!"

I tried to tell them what happened at Community Hospital. I was taken down for tests one day where I had to drink two glasses of chalk-like fluid. When the attendant picked me up on the gurney, he told the nurses that he would have me back in a couple hours!! Supposedly they were to take pictures every ten minutes for two hours after I drank the chalk-like fluid. When I got down there and the technician handed me two glasses of fluid, I said, "Do you have a diaper?" She looked me straight in the eye for several seconds and very confusedly said, "A diaper?" I said, "Yes, everything I eat goes right through me!!" She said, "No, I don't have a diaper." But after looking thoughtful a couple seconds, she said, "I will get you a towel to sit on." I said, "Okay." Then she put a towel on a *cloth* chair, gave me the two glasses of fluid, and left the room.

I drank the first glass within three minutes. I had started on the second glass when I thought, "oh oh," and I raced for the bathroom leaving a white trail from the chair to the bathroom. The nurse came back a couple minutes later, followed the white trail from the chair to the bathroom, and said, "Are you all right? What happened?" I said, "I told you. *Everything* goes right through me." She said, "Well, I am going to have to call the doctor." To make a long story short, the doctor said for her to take some pictures and send me back to my room, where the shocked nurses (I was back in less than one half hour.) had one horrible job of removing all of that *white glue* from the insides of my legs and feet!

Now, back to the camera! They told me I could have clear fluids only until 12:30, at which time I could have a light lunch. At 1230 I had a BLT and a cup of coffee. And—at 1:20 I passed the camera, *flashing brightly*! I washed it three times thoroughly in hot sudsy water, put it in a plastic sandwich bag, and went back to the hospital.

I guess I was the first one to ever return before 4 o'clock with the camera in tow! They all got a bang out of it. When I opened my purse to show them, it was still flashing away!! One nurse asked if she could take it to show the doctor. Still flashing, he found it hilarious, she said.

At any rate, they found the problem. Radiation had caused the blood vessels to come to the surface in the small intestines and they would get irritated and bleed.

I don't understand what happened, but after swallowing the camera I never did have internal bleeding again!

This past summer we went to the Cape for four months. Now that I think back on it, it was probably poor judgement! I put in a most miserable four months. My stomach was all blown up, even under the ribs. My feet and ankles were so puffed I could hardly walk. And I couldn't eat!! And such belly aches. It felt like two fists down there with very heavy pulses!!

The oncologist suggested an X-ray and a CT scan but I figured, "No, these doctors all order tests to see what is wrong but then there isn't anything they can do about it. Well, this time I was wrong! I said to the doctor up north, "These CT scans just about kill me. I suffer terribly for about three days afterwards because of the stuff you have to drink." He said, "Well, when do you go back home south?" I said, "September 28th." He said, "Then we'll wait and let your Florida doctor take care of it." (That was about the end of August or first of September.) *So I suffered on.* If he had that my stomach was full of fluids and it could be drained and I would feel a lot better afterwards, but it required a CT scan first, I would have (gladly) gone through with it.

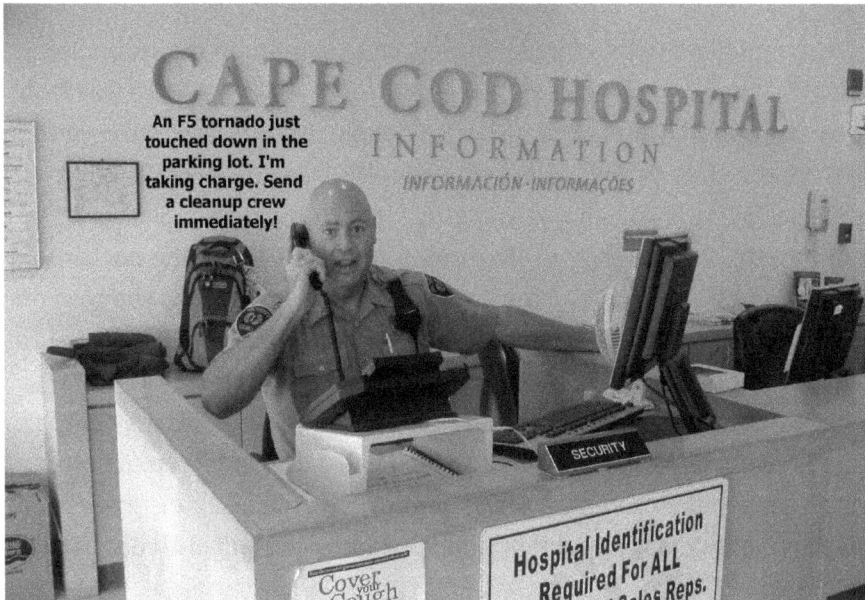

Wayne would take point in assisting the folks when they were on the Cape.

Upon my return to Florida I went to my primary care doctor right away. She ordered a CT scan immediately and then contacted my oncologist, who called me in and ordered the procedure to have the fluid drained from my abdomen. I couldn't believe how much fluid they removed: 6000 cc$_s$ (six large "soda" bottles full!!) I had to hold my stomach afterwards when I got up from the table because there was so much room in my stomach that everything was moving around and it hurt. But within a couple days, it was feeling 100% better. My stomach had solidified so that I didn't have to hold it when I got up off anything. And I could eat again—and go to the bathroom without a horrible stomach ache!

And, oh yes, I must tell you this. The CT scan also reported that I had all the symptoms of cirrhosis of the liver, so they sent me for a liver and spleen scan. I was put into the hospital overnight for this procedure because I also needed a blood transfusion. When they took me down to have the liver and spleen scan, they asked if I was able to walk over to the machine from the gurney. I said, "Yes," so I walked over to the machine with the doctor and the gurney attendant helping me. There was a board there about 12 inches wide. I said, "Oh my goodness. You expect me to lay on that narrow thing? Are you sure I won't fall off?" They assured me there was a groove in it for my feet, a pillow for my head, and I was to hold onto the sides!! I had seen so many heavy people in the hospital each time I went that I said to them, "What do you do for the fat people when they come in?" The attendant said, "WE PRAY!" I got a bang out of that; it was cute. But I never will understand why that table had to be so narrow.

This is Christmas week 2003, and I am looking forward to the holidays. I am beginning to feel almost normal again, but I still have many problems. At least I have more good days than bad days now. Our wonderful children have filled our condo with big and little gifts, even home-baked cookies, which will probably be gone before Christmas because Howard and I each sneak a few now and then.

We expect to spend Christmas by ourselves; but that is by choice, or *necessity*, I should say. Kevin offered to pick us up and take us to his place when they came to pick up Linda's mother in Seminole a day or so before Christmas, but Howard and I both feel we should not overdo it. I am still very weak and need my rest, and Howard is not that well anymore either. While we were on the Cape this summer he tried to do too much. He loves to work on the property, but now he is paying for it. His back started bothering him the last week we were there—sciatic nerve problems, very painful.

Before I forget I must tell you this one story. It is funny—but sad. While I was in the hospital in October, I called Howard one morning early and he said he was miserable! He said he put in a horrible night and didn't know what to do about it. He couldn't stand the pain any longer. He said he felt as though his foot had been cut off at the ankle, and that he should go to the Emergency Room. I told him to call Dr. Jain. So he did, and she told him to go ahead and go to the Emergency Room if he thought he should. This, he did. I guess they were pretty busy that day so he was put in a bed in the corridor. They gave him a cortisone shot in the spine; and I don't know what else they did, but he was told he couldn't drive for four hours! One of our neighbors had gone there to check on him; I had called her when he didn't answer the phone and I wanted to make sure he was all right. She checked the condo first and then went to the Emergency Room and reported in to me that he was there. She then went out and got him some kind of sandwich and drink and left him trying to go to sleep. He did fall asleep, but after an hour or so (I guess they needed the bed) they woke him up and told him he could go home! He knew he couldn't drive so he came stumbling up to my room. I was just getting out of bed to use the commode so I said, "Howard, crawl into my bed and I'll sit in the chair for a while." So he laid down on my bed and went sound asleep for TWO HOURS—hiccoughing about every four seconds (real loud too). He had had hiccoughs for a week or so. Everyone that came into the room had to laugh. They all wanted to know which one of us was the patient—and I would point to me.

When he woke up he still wasn't walking right, but insisted on driving himself home. He assured me he would be very careful, and our condo was only about one half mile away. I was so relieved when he called ten minutes later and said he was home. I had called Kevin and he came over and stayed with him until I came home the next day. He is still on pain medication but is feeling much improved. He says he should be off all pills by January. Let's hope so. Between the two of us feeling so much better, maybe 2004 will be good to us.

I am not afraid to die. I feel I have lived a good life. I have had a good husband. They don't come any better than Howard and our children all appear to be settled in and happy and healthy, despite the problems of today's world. Poor Bruce we lost in 1998. He died of a heart attack while traveling from Florida back to Utah to return to his old company. He went into a Comfort Inn in Laramie, Wyoming and told the girl at the counter that he was having chest pains, and then he collapsed. Despite the fact that he was only a couple blocks from the hospital, they were unable to save him. He was only 45! At least I know he is in another world and will never suffer again, but he was a great loss to our family and we miss him.

Since I finished the first part of my book in 1996, we have had two new members join our family. Wayne married Bridget Martin, a beautiful and talented young lady from Hyannis, in October, 2002. We were happy to have Bridget join our family. Now all of our boys are contended and happy.

In January, 1998, we were happy to welcome another grandson into our family: Oliver Walton Williams, an exciting part of the household of David and Jennifer. That makes six grandchildren for us: Christina, Michael, Rebecca, Jonathan, Spencer and Oliver. I hope it will be the last of the grandchildren for us because this world is so frightening.

I know I do not have too much longer to remain here on Earth, but I am very grateful for the life I have lived. I have been so lucky in so many ways.

And to my wonderful husband, family, and dear friends, I hope I have been a source of pleasure and comfort to you. Do not grieve over my death. Just go on and get as much pleasure as you can out of life, and remember, I will be in another world with Bruce, my mother and father, Polly, Ed, and Kenny—at peace, where I will never suffer again.

I love you all... and *you know* who *you all* are!

Pearl's Lifetime List of Medical Problems

Here, in no particular order, is a list of Pearl's medical ailments that she wrote down in the last year of her life.

Chicken Pox/Measles/Whooping Cough

Frenectomy of the upper lip (in her mid-twenties)

Cataracts

Type 2 Diabetes, which progressed from pills to insulin injections

Diabetic Retinopathy

Chronic Kidney Disease

Non-Hodgkin's Lymphoma

Bladder Infection

Irritable Bowel Syndrome

Cirrhosis (scarring) of the Liver

High Blood Pressure

Anemia

Heart Failure

Lymph Nodes under Arm

Skin Cancer: tip of nose and under eye on face

Hypothermia

Dehydration

Toxic Blood Syndrome

Degraded Mobility

Thin and Brittle Skin

Memory Loss with aging

[Despite any and all of these ailments, absent hospitalization, Pearl soldiered on with the cooking, cleaning, and general care for Howard and herself. Amazing.]

Instructions to Follow upon Death

Upon my death I request that my family and all of my good friends be notified. It is my desire that there be no service of any kind. Howard can have a Mass said for me if it makes him feel better.

It is also my desire to be cremated and put into an urn, which shall be held by Howard, or any other member of the family, if necessary, until his death, at which time I wish to be buried with Howard in, hopefully, the Osterville cemetery.

Howard can make his desires known to the children after my death, but wherever he goes, I wish to remain with him.

[Their ashes would be buried together in the Mosswood Cotuit cemetery—in the same plot as Howard's mother, Louise.]

Miscellaneous Pictures

Me, 75 years old - with new wig
During my illness I lost a total
of 100 lbs. The above picture
was taken a few months after
I started chemo when I
weighed 168 lbs. — (Today,
February 2004 I weigh 137 lbs.
I have gained 12 lbs back!)
Me, with no hair
←

[Horrible change since first book printed in 1996.]

FLORIDA TODAY, Monday, September 21, 1998

Engineer Bruce Williams, 45, dies

By Jennifer Sangalang
FLORIDA TODAY

MELBOURNE — Bruce Howard Williams, an electrical and digital communications systems engineer with AirNet Communications, P-Com and Mnemonics of Melbourne, died Friday, Sept. 18, in Laramie, Wyo., while traveling. He was 45.

Mr. Williams was born in Hackensack, N.J. He came to Brevard County in 1996 from Salt Lake City to work for small companies in the communications industry, said his brother, Kevin Williams of Orlando.

He got a jump-start in his career during his four-year service in the Air Force, where he worked with an electronics technician for the Strategic Air Command on Minuteman missiles. From there, he acquired his bachelor's degree in electrical engineering at the South Dakota School of Mines and Technology. He received his master's degree at the University of Utah.

"He had at least eight patents for extremely high-tech communications systems," Williams said.

His strong background in digital communications design, which is applicable to the technology of telephone links and high-speed communications, only increased with his more than 23 years' experience.

He had been a member of the Institute of Electrical and Electronics Engineers, Eta Kappa Nu and Tau Beta Phi since 1979.

Mr. Williams' avid interest in computers passed on to his two children.

"His kids are also computer wizards. The younger one is a demon on the computer," his brother said.

Other hobbies included hiking, bicycling, snowskiing and roller hockey. He had a big-belly laugh, enjoyed telling stories and even experimented at making beer, his brother said.

"I think that's probably what most people remember him for, his quick wit, and the fact that he liked to have a good laugh," Williams said. "He's going to be deeply missed by his family and friends; there will be a void there that's hard to fill."

He was a member of St. Joseph Catholic Church in Palm Bay.

Other survivors include his wife of 17 years, Christine Williams of Melbourne; daughter, Rebecca Williams of Melbourne; son, Jonathan Williams of Melbourne; parents, Howard and Pearl Williams of Osterville, Mass.; and brothers, David Williams of Media, Pa., Craig Williams of Falls Church, Va., and Wayne Williams of Osterville.

Calling hours will be from 5 to 8 p.m. Tuesday at Brownlie and Maxwell Funeral Home in Melbourne. Services will be at 10 a.m. Wednesday at St. Joseph Catholic Church on Babcock Street.

[New addition to the family. David's second son.]

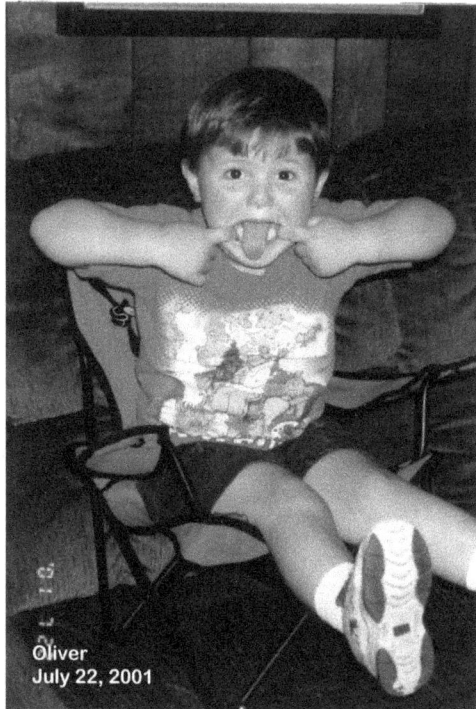

Oliver
July 22, 2001

OLIVER WALTON WILLIAMS
BORN: 1998
Oliver was told to smile!

[Wayne got married]

SUNDAY, DECEMBER 1, 2002   *Cape Cod Times*

WEDDINGS

Williams-Martin

CENTERVILLE – Bridget Ann Martin and Wayne Jonathan Williams, both of Hyannis, were joined in marriage at Our Lady of Victory Church in Centerville by the Revs. Mark Hession, Richard Wilson, Dermot Rodgers and David Frederici. A reception followed at Wequaquet Lake Yacht Club in Centerville.

The bride, daughter of Joseph Dennis Martin Jr. of Marstons Mills and the late Wilma Joyce Martin, was given in marriage by her father to the son of Howard Anthony and Pearl Marney Williams of Osterville and New Port Richey, Fla.

Linda Joyce Martin of Marstons Mills, sister of the bride, was the maid of honor. The bridesmaid was Jyoti Namita Martin of Marstons Mills, niece of the bride.

Michael Hank Williams of Falls Church, Va., served as his uncle's best man. The usher was Kerry Joseph Martin of Marstons Mills, nephew of the bride.

The bride graduated from Sacred Heart High School in 1986 and earned a bachelor's degree in Spanish from Simmons College in 1990.

R. WALTER BEDNARK

**MR. AND MRS.
WAYNE J. WILLIAMS**

She is employed as a medical secretary at Cape Cod Hospital.

The bridegroom graduated from Glebe Acres Preparatory High School in 1980, and served in the Army from 1982 to 1987. He is employed as a security officer at Cape Cod Hospital.

Mr. and Mrs. Williams honeymooned at Walt Disney World. They are residing in Hyannis.

Howard's
Graduation
Picture from
Boston
College
in 1952

HOWARD
always has
been a
lot of fun!
(OCTOBER
2002)

Howard & Pearl Williams
4939 Floramar #607
New Prt. Riche, FL 34652-3309

I LOVE FLORIDA

One thing I forgot to mention in my book: - We were so lucky to have stumbled upon this 3 bedroom, 2 bath condo at the Sea Castle in New Port Richey. - We have had such a wonderful time there. - Not only have we made the most wonderful friends in the world, but another big PLUS has been the location. The hospital and all of my wonderful doctors and nurses are all within a three - mile radius. (Don't ever let anyone fool you into thinking the doctors up North are better!) Despite some of the stories in my book, I would not hesitate to recommend any one of the Florida Doctors I have now to anyone.

I LOVE FLORIDA

Afterword

[From here on is the Afterward—written by family and friends to finish the Pearl and Howard tale.]

Parents' 50th Wedding Anniversary

David's Talk at Parents 50th Wedding Anniversary
Howard and Pearl Williams
June 9, 2001

[This is a *very* abbreviated version, as I spoke for a half hour.]

Hello everyone. I'm glad you all could come to help us celebrate Mom and Dad's 50th wedding anniversary. You'll have to bear with me. As the number three son, I don't often get a chance to speak.

How many of you here actually attended the wedding? I'm going to ask you to remember back and see if I have the story right. And correct me if I'm wrong. After the ceremony the reception was held at the Marney home on Tower Hill Road. Mom threw the bouquet and it landed on the roof. Steady young Uncle Arthur held the ladder while spry Uncle Ed nimbly dashed up to the roof. The beautiful women in their fancy dresses gathered around waiting for the flowers once again. And Ed threw them right to Sally (now his wife). She fell in love with him on the spot and has worshipped the ground he's walked on since. (He really threw them to his oldest sister, Pauline.) This is going to surprise you, but while we kids lived at home we never celebrated any of our parent's previous anniversaries. It was only after college that I even started sending cards. As I recall while growing up we'd half remember and ask if they were going to have an anniversary and they'd always say something like, "Yes, but it was two days ago." Or, "It was last week." It seemed always to be a secret. Now Dad, I'll put you on the spot because no woman would let this day pass with nothing. What did you guys do to celebrate? Did you put us to bed, bring out the champagne, and drink yourselves silly until 2 in the morning? (They claimed that they did nothing. They were too busy.) Well guess what. It may have taken 50 years but look around. The cat's out of the bag!!

Now here's a story about Mom and Dad that will shed light on how they might enjoy the unusual. They visited me in Philly twelve years ago and we went to Tom Jones Restaurant. No, not some fancy restaurant named after the Welsh Singer, just an inexpensive diner owned by some guy named Tom Jones. They ordered the baked chicken platter. It came with a baked potato and vegetable. Well when their meals came they almost fell out of their seats because the potato they each got was bigger than any that we'd ever seen. It took up over half the plate! They laughed and laughed. They couldn't get over the size of those potatoes or that anyone could serve such a potato. They doggy-bagged the bigger of the two, took it home to Virginia, and stored it in their freezer for years—showing their "nuclear" potato to anyone who visited. I think they even took it to the Cape when they retired.

Fifty years. Daunting just to think about it and how times have changed since then. Just look at one small area that I'm very familiar with having two small boys myself: cartoons, and see how they've changed.

Does anyone remember a cartoon that was introduced each time with a moose who would try to pull a rabbit out of his hat? He'd rip off his shirt cuffs saying "Nothing up my sleeve" then reach in a hat and pull out a wild boar. Anyone 40 to 55 years old probably would know what cartoon it came from. Can anyone under 35 name the cartoon? (No one could or would.) The Rocky and Bullwinkle show. How about "The Fickle Finger of Fate." I'll bet no one under 35 knows where that came from either. How about people my generation. (No one could or would. Kevin would have known but missed my talk because he was off on a wild goose chase with cousin Ricky Marney.) The answer is Rowan and Martin's Laugh-In. My generation grew up on this, and Bugs Bunny, Captain Kangaroo, Tom Terrific, and Beanie and Cecil. My younger brothers grew up on the Hanna Barbera cartoons like Yogi Bear, Quick Draw McGraw, and Snaggle Puss. They had some new cartoons too like "The Groovy Goolies". I'd notice this on the screen sometimes when the little kids were in the room and kid Wayne for years that this was his favorite one. (It wasn't')

Fifty years ago today, Mom and Dad were married right here in Osterville. And 3 years and 1 month later they had 3 boys. Almost instantly they were a family of five. I wonder if my mother knew what she was getting into when she married a Catholic. There was a 7-yr gap before Craig was born. And one and a half years later Wayne. Being curious about the 7-yr gap, I asked Mom a couple years ago why they had so many kids. Were they trying for a girl? Did they get frustrated after me and wait a while before trying again? Her answer, I think verbatim, "No, all you kids were accidents - Damn Catholics."

All of us want to thank Mom and Dad for the care they took in raising us and the help they've provided in our adult lives. (The audience was VERY restless at this point and they all thought I was finishing here. [I had been talking 15 minutes.] I thought it was hilarious—because I knew I was only halfway through. I could hear comments from my cousins. "My anniversary's coming up shortly too; please do not invite HIM!" And "Now I know why they don't let him speak!") I plowed on...

For their first 30 years they had boys in the house. I think they took one vacation by themselves in their first 7 years. Grammy came to care for Kevin, Bruce and I in Concord for that week. Where did you guys go? You must remember your one vacation. (Dad said they went to Miami.)

Dad supported all of us, played with us, went to graduate school at nights in the early years, and somehow found time to make Mom feel good about herself while tied down with all us kids. And Mom, she cut our hair, did all the shopping for the seven of us, prepared all our meals, washed all the dishes, and did all the cleanup. Plus the laundry. We never helped! My kids are going to do their own laundry as soon as I can teach them how to use the washer and dryer.

Even when Mom went back to work she continued doing all the homemaker chores. I'd come home from college and all of us men would be sitting in the family room after one of Mom's dinners and watching TV while she cleaned up the dishes. There was never a "Thank You." In fact oftentimes when she'd be putting the dishes and pots away they'd rattle and we'd look at one another and think. What the hell is wrong with her? Does she have to be that noisy? During one cleanup, I raised the question to Dad and he just threw up his hands, as if saying, "I don't know what the hell is wrong with her." We were clueless! In fairness to Dad, he may never have heard my question so he may have thrown up his hands because of that. Regardless, he was still clueless—maybe just not as much as the rest of us, especially me. I can remember coming back from college for a visit and after Mom prepared dinner thinking to myself with annoyance, "Why doesn't she set the damn table." It's been a long time but I'll say it now for all of us. Thanks, Mom! That was a lot of work.

As my kids grow up I actually think to myself if I'm doing them justice because I compare their happiness with what I had. We had true childhoods - a time that every kid should have when there isn't a worry in the world. Much of that is due to Mom and Dad. It's my theory that a happy childhood is the basis for the general feelings of "the good old days." Many people talk about "the good old days." It's a time when people were kinder and Government was wiser. In actuality, the Good Old Days has been proven to be nothing more than a myth. Each adult generation has said the young people have no respect or no manners. For my generation, the baby boomers, a lot of us wondered "Why" when younger men took to wearing earrings.

And what's with the 60 plusers. Can anyone explain black nylon knee socks with shorts and shoes. I see these old guys all the time at the shore with their bird legs and no tans. It's not attractive. (No one could explain it though one person offered that it was the Jews that do this.) But maybe it looks right to them. Everyone conforms to their own crowd.

Now I'd like to talk about my own childhood. It'll probably spark similar memories to your own. We were made to feel special growing up in that small one-bathroom ranch house on the outskirts of Concord. Looking at it now you couldn't imagine the fun we had growing up there. Busy street in front. Small front and back yards. Sloping ground behind the back yard to a thick forest. It was too secluded to go anywhere really without a car. But we had a great time. And we were there so much and my parents took so few vacations that whenever we did leave - like for two weeks to the Cape in the summer - Mom always said, "Goodbye House" as we left. And we'd all join in saying it too.

We were very active - just like my two boys - except there were five of us. What did we do? In the less cold months (because the warm months only lasted about 2 1/2 weeks back then) we played Combat and Cowboys and Indians all through the back woods. We tromped it down to make paths everywhere.

There were neighborhood kids that came to play too. Dad built a rough fort for us out of fallen trees and branches. Looked pretty professional. Called it Fort Apache. Imagine a gang of 10-year olds with stick rifles chasing after each other whooping and hollering making gunshot sounds. We had a trapeze that we'd swing on like Tarzan too. Nothing fancy, just a rope tied to a high branch halfway up the hill with a thick stick for the seat. And in the Winter, we sledded down the wooded hill in back for hours and chased each other back up - again and again. We'd come back inside exhausted, overheated, wet, and cold and Mom would always be there to give us fresh dry clothes and something to drink.

Growing up our holidays were always warm and cheery. Halloween was great fun. We'd dress up in rude costumes and come back with grocery bags full of candy. Thanksgiving, we always had a big turkey meal and a special treat - apple cider. Dad'd put it outside overnight and it'd get ice cold. The little things mattered so much more back then before today's age of instant gratification. We had cider twice a year: Thanksgiving and Christmas. Today, our kids drink cider - three gallons a week, rain or shine, Winter, Spring, Summer or Fall. Of course Christmas was the pinnacle of the year for us. Excitement would build for months - and Santa was always very good to us.

Concord itself had its benefits with its rich history and added to our feelings of being special. As cub scouts we'd get up at dawn and gather with the troop at the Old North Bridge to reenact with cannon the shot heard round the world that symbolized the start of the Revolutionary War. We'd visit the "Bullet Hole House." Years later I'd come to appreciate this history. Henry David Thoreau spent his well-known time in solitude in the woods of Walden. Does anyone know what book he wrote afterwards? "Self-Reliance." It comes up in conversation every so often and I enjoy telling people that I had swimming lessons there, at Walden Pond.

Cape Cod was magical too when we'd come here visiting the relatives in the summer. Grammy Marney had an open door policy and we'd all come and go as we pleased. Some people might see it as a chore—watching kids. But she truly enjoyed us and the fun that we had. Nana Williams was very nice too. She provided for us without complaint, took us blueberry picking, and took us on long rides. She used to braid rugs and spent hours at it. We'd see her hunched over on her knees stitching the braids together. I have one of her colorful rugs in my bedroom. Every now and then I'll look down on it and think of her.

Swimming in Joshua's pond, fishing in Mike's pond, Craigville and Dowses Beaches, movies at the Osterville Theater for 50 cents, Uncle Kenny's packing all of us kids in his jeep and taking us to the Four Seas for ice cream. All these made for wonderful memories.

We moved a couple times after Concord. After 8th Grade we moved to Clearwater, Florida. Upon graduating High School, my parents moved to McLean, Virginia. The last of the kids flew the coop around 1981. Only 10 more years of outside work remained. Then Mom and Dad retired: "No more homework, no more books, no more bosses dirty looks." That was in 1991 and they've enjoyed 10 years retirement so far. Is life really that short? It didn't seem that way when we were living it.

My brothers and I want to thank Mom and Dad for the wonderful childhoods they gave us and for the help they've given us afterwards. Those early years and their working years were full, busy, happy, stressful - everything. We've very happy that you finally retired and have had 10 years so far to do whatever you've wanted to do—and to relax. Happy Anniversary!

Pearl's Death through Cancer

Note: I originally offered this story to the Cape Cod Times hoping they would run segments over a several week period as a general interest article on Cape Cod native sons.

Dear Sir,

I'm offering a feature article that may be of interest to your readers. This is the story of my parents, a Cape Cod couple who married, cared for one another, and faced old age, cancer, and Alzheimer's together. It is also a son's reflections on the sacrifices of parenthood, the losses of parents, even when they lead long rich lives, and what makes people unique.

They declined.

Pearl (Marney) Williams, my mother, passed away this June 8th, 2010. She was 83. An Osterville native (with many Marneys still living on the Cape) and 1945 graduate of Barnstable High School, she had been fighting Non-Hodgkin's Lymphoma for eight years.

Although she didn't look it, especially in the later years, Mum (that's what we called her) was a tough old bird. When I was six and she a 33 year old mother of three, I remember her sitting in the kitchen slightly out of breath telling us that she had just come up from doing laundry in the basement where she had stepped on a board with nails sticking out of it. (Expecting more children, Dad had been finishing part of the basement for an extra bedroom.) We all went downstairs for a closer look. Sure enough, there was the offending board, with two wicked looking finishing nails sticking out of it about a half inch apart. We followed the trail of twin blood dots leading up the stairs. Mum went to get a tetanus shot, but what amazed me was how calm she was throughout. She didn't make a peep. I didn't like stepping on a pebble, and couldn't imagine the pain of a nail puncturing through the sole of my foot.

True to form, in her late 70's Mum would choose aggressive cancer treatment. It wasn't only for herself, it was for Dad's sake too (explanation to follow). So she endured a rigorous schedule of Chemo and Radiation therapy. The unfortunate side effects were that some of her bodily systems (including her liver) were damaged permanently. Her weakened digestive tract required her to maintain umbilical cord proximity to restroom facilities forever after. No more travel for her (and she loved visiting family) and only short trips for necessary shopping.

Her circulatory system didn't function well either. Her bone marrow could no longer produce enough red blood cells to maintain her strength. To compensate, she took Procrit injections. This gave an almost magical energy boost. But she required more and more injections as time went on. Transfusions as well. These became less and less effective. During the last year, she was up to one transfusion per month and sometimes two Procrit injections per week – at $700.00 per injection. But without it, life wouldn't have been livable. Fortunately, Mum's Government Service retirement benefits were most generous. Otherwise it would have cost a mini fortune – just for the Procrit. What do people do who don't work for the government, or who have poor or (gasp) no health insurance?

On the subject of politics Mum was a Democrat but she loved to watch conservative Fox News and the cable networks for their outspoken opinionated coverage. The McLaughlin Group round table of shouting heads was particularly entertaining. She listened to these shows a lot but Mum had many opinions that were her own, and she was willing to express them. On the Kennedy's, whom she supported wholeheartedly, she told me once that while they may have been bad for their own women at times, they were great for (all) women all the time.

She came a long way from the shy daughter of an Osterville village carpenter and family farmer who kept most thoughts to herself. In the beginning she was so shy that after she was dropped off her first day in kindergarten she cried the whole day. This changed after marriage. It had to. She would have her first child, Kevin, within one week after her nine month wedding anniversary. (They were married on June 9, 1951.) There would be two more boys born in quick succession: Bruce and then me, David. The three of us were one school year apart from each other, and very close. Seven years would pass and two more boys, Craig and Wayne, would be born, again each one grade apart.

We would be called the "big kids" and the "little kids," and we all needed the usual demanding parental attention. It was up to Mum to step up since Dad was working as a mechanical engineer during the day and attending graduate school at night. He would complete a master's degree in mechanical engineering and a Juris Doctor in Law. Mum became the center of our attention and our leader. She fed us, cleaned up after us, bathed us, refereed our battles, nursed our wounds, and put us to bed. You can't be shy when you're doing everything full time for your kids – especially when there are three of them so close in age. She became independent, evolving definite opinions on household rules and children's behavior. The opinions expanded to include home decoration and landscaping. And no doubt about it, she made the major decisions on all these subjects in the family.

Bruce, Kevin, David circa 1956

Wayne and Craig in the Spring of 1967

We kids were conditioned to follow our parents and to respect our elders. We were subordinate to adults—all adults. Every grownup in authority had infinite wisdom in comparison to ours. As elementary schoolers, there were a few occasions where we had cause to complain about some injustice committed against us by a teacher. Three to one, we'd argue our case but Mum never took our side. I know now that she wanted the issue to go away rather than to continue a no win situation with authority. So after a short vigorous argument where no end appeared in sight, Mum would pull out the old trump card and deliver it at high volume. The teacher was right "because she is an aaa-dult." And that would be it. What could we say? She was pretty old after all. There were only a handful of these occasions, and none of them were serious. Mum was following her small town moral compass which valued respect and support for authority.

We were raised with the adage "Children should be seen and not heard." It was a nice try, but we were loud—very loud. Our next door neighbors would tell us years later that they even contemplated moving because of our noise. But we weren't noisy to spite anyone. We would never even have thought of challenging Mom and Dad's authority. They said "Get into the car. We're going to the dump." We got in the car! Today, I say to my kids "Get into the car. We're going to the swimming pool." Big argument! We of the baby boom generation notice this all the time. (Sigh!)

Mum's independence in landscaping was kind of funny though, and would lead to a chink in the parental armor. She preferred the "overgrown look"—to put it mildly. They planted a lot of trees and shrubs, and lo and behold, they grew. The formula was always the same: One third old soil, one third new top soil and one third Bo-Vung (Bovine Dung) fertilizer. I sometimes watch reality shows where they flip houses for resale. They do the exact opposite of what Mum did. They professionally landscape the property; they eliminate overgrowth; they get curb appeal. That's what sells! When the "little kids" reached high school age, Craig and Wayne saw a need to act. They found it difficult to mow the lawn under all the branches and long limbed bushes. So, many times when my parents left for a weekend vacation, they trimmed trees and bushes—sometimes like mad. Frequently, Mum noticed and loud one-sided arguments ensued. But many times she overlooked it. (The property was still overgrown after all.) We "big kids" took it that Mum and Dad had mellowed with age. The "little kids" had it a lot easier.

Although she overcame her childhood shyness, Mum never lost her childhood values. I know people respected authority more in "the good old days" but surely not as much as Mum. She never laid her hands on us or used a switch. She controlled us with her voice—which could get loud. We lived nearby to a state penitentiary in those days, and when pushed to the limit she used to say "I'd rather see you dead than in jail." I wish I could remember what we kids were doing that caused her to issue this dire warning. I'm sorry Mum, if we drove you right to the edge at times.

Mum retained her country mannerisms throughout life too. Her conversations often remained laced with small town colloquialisms. If we asked for too much, as kids do, she might direct us to "Take a back seat." As adults, regardless of age, if we reached an impasse on a personal matter and all reason was exhausted, you might hear a final "Don't you fool yourself!" But there was never any doubt that she wanted what was best for us. She was our Mum.

Through the years all her boys would settle down in different states. We didn't want to. It just worked out that way. Fortunately, at least we remained mostly on the East Coast. As single young adults we always gathered together at Christmastime. Even afterwards it was a rare year when we didn't visit at least once – though never all the boys at the same time. Mum was a great one for keeping contact over the phone too. We'd call at home, but I'll admit too that many of us called weekly (at least) at her credit union workplace – where she could be reached via a "free" 800 number used by the tens of thousands of investors. (A hidden cost of hiring a mother with grown kids.) When they returned in retirement to Cape Cod in 1991 we always tried to vacation with them at least once at their Osterville home. The Cape was our home too after all the weekly summer visits to our grandparents during childhood.

Despite Mum giving her all against Cancer, it caught up to her - it almost always does. The only thing keeping her going near the end was her family. We'd call and her frail sounding voice would answer the phone. (Why Dad never answered will become clear later.) Thinking we'd better keep the call short, to our amazement she usually perked up and gained strength. We'd talk for half an hour! But the last month had shown that the end was near. With a long standing DNR request (Do Not Resuscitate) she was in and out of ambulances and hospitals. Her liver and kidneys were shutting down. Potassium and Ammonia were building up in her blood. (Who knew to expect this?) The imbalances caused her to faint. When she stirred to bare consciousness she was still helpless. We were all very fortunate that she retained her strength and reason to put her final affairs in order and to say her last goodbye's. When she died, peacefully, under doctor's medicated care in a hospice, we all knew it was a blessing. And we took comfort in the fact that she was at peace.

Howard's Demise through Alzheimer's

But this story is equally about Dad—Howard Williams. A quick family background is that Dad's father, Francis, suffered a stroke in the late afternoon of 22 March, 1944 while shoveling his car out of a snowbank. A 16 year old Howard would sit with his father by his hospital bed as he drew his last breath. The death certificate would list it as a Spontaneous Cerebral Hemorrhage. Even in his 60s, Howard admitted to family members that he never got over this loss.

Louise Riedel (Howard's mom) 1922

His mother, Louise (Riedel) Williams moved the family from Dorchester, MA to Osterville, Cape Cod where she had a brother and two sisters. For two decades, starting in 1947, she worked as a nurse at Cape Cod Hospital. And she never remarried. About her siblings, brother Carl Riedell (He added an extra L to the name) would start a plumbing business that still carries on today. Sisters Tina and Margaret were married to Jesse Murry and "Mutt" McGoff, respectively. Family offspring would unite with the Farrington and Thomas families. There were many cousins and second cousins. During high school, Dad worked for Uncle Jesse's business delivering ice that they chopped out of Joshua's pond and stored in an ice house there. This was before the age of common electric refrigeration.

Amongst this large extended family, Howard would start 11th grade in Barnstable High School and graduate in 1946. He played baseball and football. He even became the Senior Class President. Most importantly, he met Mum there. While dating, he would call her the Pearl of Osterville.

Pearl at age 19

Without going into more detail about his professional career and later family life, Dad has been struggling with Alzheimer's for the past four years. Mum had been his primary care giver all that time, allowing him to continue living at home. Medicine had slowed the disease's progress, but Alzheimer's, like growing old, never stops. Without dear old Mum helping with day to day guidance, the family, (sons Kevin, David (me), Craig and Wayne) would have had to find Dad full time care at least one year ago, and probably two. (Note: Second son, Bruce, had died suddenly of a blood clot at the age of 45 on 9/18/1998. That was our family's 9/11.)

Mum had always been worried about what would happen to Dad after she died. That's partly why she chose such aggressive cancer treatment. She needed to survive him. In the beginning she used to worry that he would remarry and squander our inheritance that they had both built up on the new wife and family. This happens more often than you'd think. (What's with these old goats?) This worry evaporated with Dad's advancing condition. Then a new worry arose. Who would care for Dad if she were gone?

She did some personal writing in her retirement years and wrote that when her time was near, and if Dad was in bad straights, she would go to the garage with him, shut the door, get in the car, start it up, open the windows, and they'd both breathe in the carbon monoxide and go to sleep – for keeps. I asked Mum what Dad, a good practicing Catholic, said about this. She said that he knew of her plans, and that he never agreed. But he never said no to her either. She took this as quiet consent. In fact, later on, Mum and I would discuss this right in front of him - while he still had his faculties. Sure enough, he said not a word.

It shouldn't have surprised me that Mum knew him best. If she had lived one more day, they would have been married for 59 years. For all that time she took care of him. She did all the cooking and all the cleaning. He was the breadwinner, but she helped with the finances by going back to work when the "little kids" reached high school. But I don't recall Dad taking that much time off either. He'd watch TV with us in the family room after dinner while Mum put away the dishes and loaded up the dishwasher. When she finished, he'd retire with her to the living room. They'd lie down on the same couch, each one with a head at an opposite end. With their feet in each other's laps they'd comfort one another. And they'd talk and talk until time for bed. All through college I'd come home and the routine never varied. Except that I'd join them in the living room and talk to them too, about school at the University of Virginia or life in general. At one time all three *big kids* attended UVA.

David, Kevin, Bruce July 1955

Dad had always been a complex fellow. He was private, yet he could be boisterous at times too. He was wonderful with small kids. I can remember him picking us up by the feet and carrying us off laughingly to put us to bed. Mum played into this too. When he came home from work she'd say "Daddy's home" and we'd all run to meet him and throw ourselves in his arms.

As young tykes, we had been watching cartoons one Saturday morning and Superman or Hercules had manifested super strength by pushing over and uprooting a tree. We kids started chattering excitedly when Dad piped up "What do you mean? I can do that too." Of course we didn't believe him. So he said he'd prove it in the woods behind our back yard. We were amazed as he pushed over several trees (rotten) and flexed his muscles. In our eyes, he was a hero too.

**Spring 1967 Wayne and Craig with Kevin in back seat and
Bruce in middle seat**

Dad enjoyed life and saw the humor in the life around him. He told me once about a 10K road race he had observed with my two younger brothers when they lived in McLean, Virginia, just outside of DC. He drove to the steepest part of the race—to watch the runners struggle their hardest. At this point Dad noticed two men running together. They both had thick runner's legs, but one was real tall while the other was short. Because he was Dad, he nicknamed them "Mutt and Jeff". They appeared to be competing against each other, the shorter one's legs pumping like mad to keep slightly ahead. Dad drove to the finish line to see the end. He wasn't disappointed. They both came chugging up together. But "Jeff's" legs were too long and he got ahead. Passing the finish line first, "Jeff" looked back hollering a triumphant "Gotcha!"

Dec 1992

Dad had a unique way with words. My brother Bruce was an accepting lovable fellow who attracted friends effortlessly. Animals loved him too. In Virginia, our next door neighbor was a large middle aged German fellow who worked at the

German Consulate in DC. He had a huge German Sheppard. Although "Bruno" was friendly enough, he was a rough looking dog. We all played with him, but only Bruce played rough with him. Bruno would jump up at him and Bruce would hip check him like in hockey. Then they'd wrestle. And Bruno loved it! Dad noticed this animal attraction and labeled the charisma forever after as "odeur de Bruce."

Our 7506 Box Elder Ct, McLean, VA home almost 20 years after we sold it. Professional landscaping turned it into a luxury home. (Who knew?)

Here's the backyard—a garden oasis.

The McLean House a couple years after we moved in.

1983: Howard and Wayne demonstrating how our ancestors arrived from Portugal !

Dad's words sometimes carried an edge. After a discussion with Mum, Dad once said to me with a weary voice "David, your mother has no opinions, just facts! (I had to give him sympathy there.) When they sold their McClean, Virginia home, brother Craig remained living nearby in Falls Church. Whenever any of us visited we always stopped by the old house. Usually we took pictures. Well, two doctors bought the place and they re-landscaped totally. Out went most of the bushes and all the overgrowth. In went new bushes, in new locations, and in went a new fence. It looked like a house in a resort magazine. I would show the pictures to Dad and he agreed that it indeed looked beautiful. *"Sickeningly beautiful,"* he said. Actually, we both were pretty happy that the property could look so good.

About the McLean property, it may not have been a showplace but it was designed for fun growing up. We played a lot of croquet and badminton in the backyard. Killer badminton, as I recall—lotta slams. We also had a great above the ground pool. Several of us would start running in circles inside and get the water to form a vortex; then let it float us around. If Mom weren't careful one of us would give her a nudge—and she'd take a ride with us!

I'll preface these next comments by admitting that all my family, excepting Mum, loved teasing one another. Dad's teasing often took the form of sentences that had double meanings, one normal and one *different*. If he stopped the car too abruptly he might say "The car stopped with a jerk, and out stepped David." (Huh?) If one of us did something clever and we were overly proud he might say "Well, you're no ordinary fool." (What?) If one of my brothers passed gas (ahem) he might volunteer "Your voice is changing, but your breath is still the same." (Is that so?) Or if a foul odor of unknown origin wafted across the room and you complained, his sympathy might consist of "It's probably just your own breath blowing back in your face."

When we got older, if we spoke too fast or got too excited, he'd imitate us with gibberish like "ooba dabba dooba dabba." He'd use the same inflections and pace that we'd used. Many times one or more of us would respond with his gibberish right back at him. Then we'd look at each other and we'd all laugh. And I don't want to forget that when he sneezed, he gave an ear splitting "rue - SHAW!" That was Dad. I could go on and on.

In reflecting on the idiosyncrasies, I may not have expressed very well the dignity that Dad possessed; it was a lot. He was extremely honest, probably the most honest person I've ever met. He's one of the few people who never cheated on his taxes. And I'd bet that he never (and I mean never) missed a week without going to church. But he was comical as well. It was an engaging mix.

One final thought, Dad had a habit of giving waitresses fits using humor. I can't remember exactly what he did, but I remember the rest of us would cringe in our seats. He'd trouble her with odd requests, perhaps with double meanings, and challenge her to handle him. But his humor wasn't common, obvious or crass, and he normally got away with his cleverness. He was always searching for the waitress who could handle him. Oddly enough, he found her - frequently. (It helped that he wanted them to win.)

But Alzheimer's would curb most of his humor. It's tough to be Don Rickles (acerbic comedian) when the synapses slow down, or they no longer reach the necessary store of memories. We couldn't help but notice a slowing of his mental processes. It started with a decrease in his e-mails. He used to be big on this, sending out at least several per month, more during family crises.

Howard at age 50

****
Here's a couple of his e-mails.

November 30, 2001

Hello, Everyone,

I am scheduled to go into Bayonet Point Hospital on Wednesday, Dec.5, at 9:30 AM, for surgery again on my right carotid artery. It was first performed in October 2000 but has filled to 98% plaque blockage as of last week. I go in for PreOp on Tuesday, December 4, at 1;00 PM for blood test and consultation. I expect to be released three days after the operation - on Saturday, December 8. The same doctor that operated this past August on my left carotid artery will be operating. The left carotid artery tested good as of last week.

I have had 18 Chelation treatments to help remove the plaque but I will be stopping further treatments because they are slow in giving good results. I expect to restart them several months after the operation.

All for now, Dad/Poppop

January 18, 2006

Dear Folks, I had some bad luck last 7 January, a Saturday. I was attending 4 pm Mass when I fainted just as the service ended! I had been standing in the back for about an hour and came to laying on the floor with two people holding my legs up high and a doctor (a parishioner) was asking me for my home phone number. I gave it to him and he asked someone to call for an ambulance and to notify Pearl! I had no pain but was very weak. The ambulance came and took me to the Community Hospital less than a mile away.

After about 5 hours in the admittance room, I was assigned a bed! I went through EEG, chest X-rays, blood tests, etc. until 10 January I was taken to an operating room to have a Pacemaker installed. It was supposed to last only 1.5 hours but one of the device's two leads to my heart - the upper chamber lead - was found to be insecure so the operation was extended an extra hour so this could be fixed.

I was released on Thursday, 12 January, with a belt sling to hold my left arm against my stomach to prevent any movement that might dislodge the 3 inch Pacemaker. Son Kevin came over from Orlando to help Pearl and me. I cannot drive until the doctor OKs it, hopefully this Friday. Pearl is chauffeuring both of us around until I drive again. She is a bit wary since she has depended on me for the past three years to take her to doctors, shopping, etc.

I feel much better now although I can't play golf again for about 10 weeks!

Regards to all, Howard & Pearl

****

The flow of e-mails diminished drastically after Dad got his pacemaker in January 2006. In hindsight, this was a clear indicator that he was suffering some beginnings of dementia. He started forgetting how to use the computer. It was more than the usual *Windows Operating System* problems. He'd forget how to turn it on, how to log on, how to access e-mail, how to locate files, and how to print. And unlike later losses of skills that Mum could help cover for, she couldn't help with this because she had never learned to use the computer herself. Someone always helped

Mum with the few e-mails that she wrote. Dad would write one e-mail in March, 2006 and another in July, 2006. Then – no more. This would prove a harbinger for the shrinking of his world.

By the summer of 2007, Dad struggled keeping up with the usual family banter. We often teased each other when we visited, confident in our familial bonds. And, because he carried so much respect, Dad's teasing was most effective. Even when he'd lose, he'd win, if you know what I mean. But there came a time when he became a step slow and he must have realized that he couldn't participate in this fun anymore. Someone would say something funny and the wheels would turn, "Why didn't I say that?" It was a shame really. At least the waitresses could now breathe a sigh of relief.

Then this past year the disease accelerated. He would accept us when Mum welcomed us through the door, but I don't think he really knew who we were. (What was he thinking when we greeted him with big hugs.) He started forgetting immediate conversations too. He'd ask the same questions four times in a half hour. Mum answered each question as brand new. My middle school-age kids and I played along. Although it was sad, we made a game out of it. I was happy just to talk to him. But he was conscious enough to know that something was wrong. Maybe he could feel the Déjà Vu. Anyway, he would initiate conversations less and less out of fear that he would be repeating himself. And he talked less and less. I suspect this is the way Alzheimer's patients generally behave. They almost never initiate conversations and their responses are brief. I call them "the quiet ones".

In reality, Mom and Dad have been steadily slowing down for the last ten years. When they first retired in 1991, they sold the McClean, VA house and bought two smaller houses, one in Osterville and one in New Port Richey, FL. (Mum loved Florida from the four years we lived in Clearwater when the I was in high school.) Initially they drove from one home to the other. It was a four day trip during which they'd stop off and visit with me outside of Philadelphia and Craig in Falls Church, Virginia. After several years they cut me out of the loop, saying that I was too close to Craig, and they needed to shorten the trip. I argued what was the rush. Enjoy the trip. Take it easy. They were in their mid-70s at the time, and their minds were made up. I accepted it. A couple years later they would stop visiting Craig as well, because they no longer drove to Florida and back. The driving was too much. They flew, and maintained a car at each location. One more limitation occurred in the last three years. They would still make the flight to their homes but Kevin would accompany them on the plane.

Aside from travel assistance, Mum and Dad have required more and more help in general over the last three years. Oldest brother Kevin, and wife Linda, would take the lead. Kevin would visit frequently when they were in Florida, making the 2-

hour trip from his house in Orlando. Youngest son Wayne, who works at the Cape Cod Hospital, would help when they were on the Cape.

At the end, Mum and Dad were staying at the Florida home. We were still phoning. Mum would never volunteer Dad's condition, but I noticed he wasn't getting on the phone any more. I asked her. She told me that Dad was bad - much worse than the previous summer. She relayed that Dad had forgotten much of his past. Mum would tell Dad, "We had five sons." Dad, "No. I never had any kids." And although he recognized Kevin and Linda by sight, he was clueless of the relationships. He'd ask, "Who is that man driving me around?" Mum, "That's Kevin, your son." Dad, "No, he's not my son. Dad, "Who's the woman with him." Mum, "His wife Linda." Dad, "No, they aren't married." He saw Kevin as Mum's friend who was helping to care for them and Linda as an attractive female who was helping clean up around the house, and also caring for them.

Dad's mind wasn't readily accepting new memories well either. Just sitting there he looked normal and he responded to conversation. It's just that he couldn't remember the details, like his own birth date or the names of towns or streets where he lived. We were lucky that he was agreeable. He'd already passed the frustration stage in Alzheimer's where he'd get upset when he got confused. Mum saw him through that stage all by herself - and handled it with patience. While we cared for him, he'd eat what was set in front of him, he'd help clean up, and he'd go with us to run errands. He could even drive the car (a scary thought and something we prevented.) But he needed someone in the car with him because he never would have found his way back. In fact, he couldn't remember the name of the Sea Castle housing complex where he lived in New Port Richey, Florida.

May 30, 2010

With Mom in the hospital and then hospice care, cousin Janet flew in to New Port Richey to care for Dad, staying nine days.

He did seem to enjoy our company. But his brain was resetting every 15 minutes. It was during this stage in Dad's degeneration that Mum passed out while getting out of their bed. And Dad didn't know what to do. A neighbor happened by an hour later. She asked "Where's Pearl? Dad's reply? "She's lying on the floor." Kevin and Linda would stay with them more and more after this, taking yet more time off from work. Cousin Janet (Williams) Bare volunteered to help, as she had done in the past. She flew in from Arizona and stayed a week, helping Kevin and Linda who continued to visit frequently. [When she read this she looked at me and said, "It was *nine days*." Bless you, Janet.] Brother Craig flew in next from Virginia and offered additional care to that of Kevin and Linda who were now staying there fulltime. It was during this time that Mum would take her last breath.

During Mum's last emergency trip to the hospital, the doctors gave her as much encouragement as possible. But recognizing what wasn't being said she knew that she wasn't going to improve. And her present state was unendurable. She decided to go to a hospice where they could help manage her death. She decided no more food and no more water. She told Dad that it was time for her to go to heaven. Dad looked at her "Aren't you going to take me with you?"

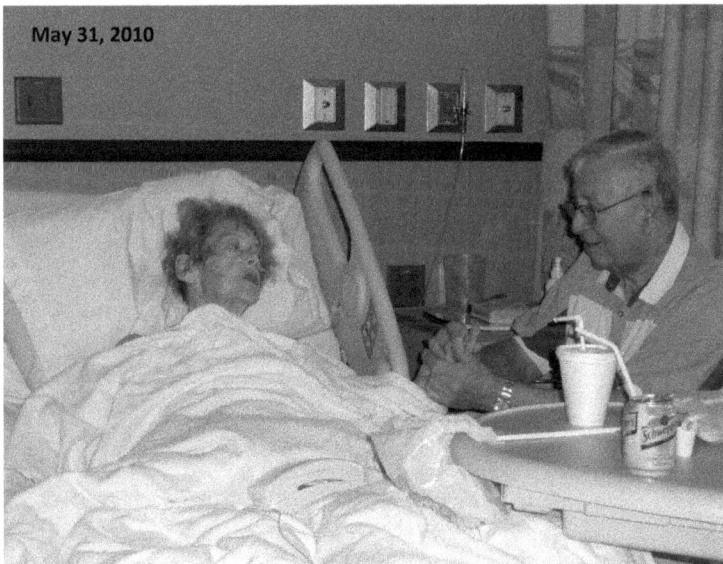

May 31, 2010

At the hospice she made sure that she had her final conversations with her sons. Mum didn't want me or Wayne to fly down. By the time we got there she didn't expect that she'd be conscious. Kevin and Craig were there. They were taking care of Dad. Living at a distance, Mum and I had always had more of a phone relationship than an in-person one. The same with Mum and Wayne. We were all very comfortable with this. We found that you don't need physical presence to show love or to remain a part of someone's life. She was a great sounding board and I could confide almost anything with her. I did visit with her at least once a year. We made our tearful goodbyes over the phone. Mum was happy (if that word applies.) And I was happy to remember her in healthier days.

Kevin, Linda and Craig drove Dad to the hospice frequently. Mum and Dad would hold hands and talk, as they had for decades on the couch. These were touching moments. There were some comical moments too. Mum was lying flat in bed conserving all her energy. She looked wiped out. No food plus no water equals no energy. Dad reached over and tried to push a few strands of hair from her face. His hand slipped and he brushed too close to her eyes. She reared up from seeming near death, "Are you trying to kill me?" Then she went back to resting. Craig and Dad could only just look at each other.

You might ask, what happened about Mum's plans with the carbon monoxide in the garage. In the end those plans turned out to be fantasy. This isn't to say that she didn't intend to follow through. Her will to live might have proved too strong. She may have reconsidered how it might reflect on the family. Her illnesses might have made her too weak to act. It may have been the simple reason that their final home in Florida didn't have an enclosed garage. We like to think that in the end she realized that she loved Dad just too much to cause him any harm.

June 3, 2010

Craig would fly in during Mom's final days, spell Janet, and fly Dad back to Falls Church, VA to stay with his family after Mom's death.

Mum would slip further and further away. She had the phone right by the bed. We'd call – even after we'd said our final goodbyes. There came a time though when the nurse disconnected the phone – because Mum could no longer answer. As much as possible, Kevin, Linda, Craig, and Dad maintained a vigil. Wayne would call the floor nurse to get the daily status. I was waiting for the inevitable call. This finally happened a couple days later, at 1:30 in the morning. It was over. She passed away on June 8, 2010, one day shy of her 59th wedding anniversary.

To my Howard?

The time is near
But I'm still hear
Thinking of the end, I fear.

I want you to know
Before I go
That I really do love you so!

Now that I have said it,
And you have read it.
I bid my adieu.
With fond memories
And everlasting love for you.

During Mom's last month, we four surviving sons knew we had to do something about poor old Dad. He could no longer live alone. Kevin and Linda took the lead again. They researched dementia facilities in Florida and Cape Cod. These were the locations that Mum felt that Dad should spend his last years. They visited several facilities in Florida. I visited a facility in Pennsylvania. We checked prices in Massachusetts and Virginia too. There was a cost range from roughly $4,000 to $6,000 per month. The Florida facilities appeared to be about $1000 cheaper than the northern ones.

The placement decision was not an easy one. A major consideration was that we wanted him close to at least one of us so that we could visit frequently. We also knew that he wouldn't recognize us as his family. Would our visits help him, or merely console us? As difficult as it was, we had to accept that wherever he went, the caregivers at the facility, along with the other guests, would become his new family. But time was running out. After visiting scores of facilities in Florida with Mom and Dad prior to Mom's death, Kevin and Linda continued to look, sometimes with Dad, and they fell in love with the Arden Courts Alzheimer's facility in St Pete,

Florida. They had done the due diligence comparison shopping. We accepted their judgment.

Before taking him there, Craig wanted one more chance for Dad to visit with him in Virginia. He had been caring for him for the last week in Florida. And Dad was acting better. Craig even let Dad drive the car at times. The thinking was that additional stimulation from Craig's family might offer improvement. They flew back to Falls Church, VA where Dad was reacquainted with Craig's wife Mandy, their two children, Chrissy and Michael, and their dog Schotzi.

Arriving in the afternoon, Dad settled in very well. His mental capacity may have decreased but he was agreeable. He enjoyed everyone's company. He seemed to remember Chrissy best. After five sons, she was the first granddaughter. He

June 14, 2010 at Craig's house with Schatzi

bonded with her through her childhood (Michael too) and it must have stuck somehow. He had a great time playing with Schotzi too, He even laid down on the floor with her.

Craig's family would make an important discovery that might have explained why Dad's condition had accelerated so much in the past two years. They watched him take his daily pills, one of which was Aricept®, a drug that impedes the symptoms of Alzheimer's. He put all his pills, at least ten, in a glass. He filled it with water. Then he drank the water. An inspection of the glass revealed a huge gob of sticky pills at the bottom!!! They retrained him on how to take his pills. But the damage was done. Who knows how long he'd been neglecting his medicine. (Kevin advised me that he and Linda were meticulous in administering the pills. But how careful was a weakened Mom in her final year as Dad's caregiver?)

It turns out that Alzheimer's is a fickle disease. The next morning, despite a great previous day, Dad told everyone that it was time for him to go home. When your brain is resetting every fifteen minutes, the visit may have felt like weeks to him. They stalled him. They encouraged him to stay. The next day he got his bags and sat outside the door waiting to be driven to the airport. He asked to telephone Kevin. They talked. Everyone tried to discourage him. The simple fact that he didn't know that he could make his own reservations and call a taxi proved that he was not capable of going home. The stalling game lasted almost a week and was stressful. Craig would not use the strongest argument against him – that if we sent him away we would not take him home. He would go to a dementia nursing facility.

Life is funny. Dad enjoyed his time at Craig's house. They ate all their meals together. They took walks and drives in the car. Craig's family made sure that someone was always present so that when Dad's brain reset he wouldn't worry that he was abandoned. Craig's mother-in-law came over to help when everyone else had to work. It was an excellent support system. Families are supposed to look out for their own. But there came a time when they could no longer stall his requests to go home. The brothers had some long talks over the phone. I would drive down from Pennsylvania on a Saturday and Craig and I would escort Dad on a plane back to Florida that afternoon. I wasn't there to help personally with Mom. I needed to help with Dad.

June 13, 2010 at Craig's house with Christina

Arriving at Craig's house that Saturday morning everyone seemed happy, including Dad. He accepted me readily, although I'm sure he didn't understand the relationship. We all sat in the family room and talked. Dad talked too, though he would remain skimpy on facts. But most of the time it was Craig and I talking. We talked about Mom passing away, and her wishes. Dad said It was very sad. We spoke about the Cape Cod house. He volunteered "Wayne's supposed to take care of the

Cape house." We made small talk. If you didn't know what to look for, or didn't know him from before, you might not notice anything wrong. But he had been a "big bucket brain" person. He could take in many facts, word them into complicated propositions, and form persuasive arguments. He had been a lawyer and had passed the Massachusetts bar. But how much remained of him now. We didn't know.

After a few hours it was time to drive out to National Airport. Dad turned to me and asked if he (Craig) were coming with us. He must have associated me and my arrival with escorting him to Florida. I told him the three of us were going. Mandy and Chrissy drove us out. During the drive, he asked again if "he" was going with us. Running a little late Craig started to worry that we hadn't left soon enough to make it through security. To save time due to the congestion we decided to offload a couple hundred yards out. We lugged our bags and continued to talk. Dad and I lagged behind while Craig charged ahead. Dad asked again "Is he coming with us?" Answering yes, I considered that Craig had been Dad's constant companion for the past two weeks. Craig occasionally turned back and exhorted us to hurry. Feeling harried, I turned to Dad and asked, "Is he always this gruff?" There was a pregnant pause when I thought he wasn't going to answer. Just as I was about to turn away, he responded, "I don't know. It's the first time I've been with him." ... Dad's brain had reset.

Despite Dad's confusion, he usually hid it well. He followed us competently through the airport and we boarded. We couldn't get three seats together because the reservation was made on short notice. We did have two seats together and Craig graciously allowed me to sit with Dad for his final plane ride. I took the middle seat and gave him the aisle. The trip was uneventful except for one circumstance. Halfway through the two hour flight, Dad and I mentioned the house on Cape Cod. A lady in her 60's sitting in the aisle seat opposite perked up at this. The flight had originated in Boston where she had boarded and she had a Cape Cod background. She wanted to talk to Dad. It became uncomfortable quickly. When Dad didn't keep up his end of the conversation she decided to help him by asking leading questions. (Horrors.) When he struggled over details, I joined in. I wanted to somehow call her off but there was no easy way to do this. It probably only lasted five minutes but it seemed an eternity. She must have noticed my anxiety and had the good manners to back out graciously.

Kevin and Linda met us at Tampa airport and we all drove to the Sea Castle condominium. I wondered how Dad would react to being home. After all, he had exhibited some stress in asking to go home. But upon entering the house, there was no unusual happiness. It was if he had just returned from a short drive. With his mind constantly resetting, maybe this is what he thought. He did know his way naturally around the house. And he seemed comfortable. It was not a pleasant thought that we were going to uproot him from his home the very next day.

We would go out to dinner that night at Carrabba's Italian Grill in Port Richey. Looking at the menu, we helped Dad decide what he wanted, thinking he could order when it was his turn. But he struggled. We gave him time to recover. It was painful—and we had to help him. It was quite a bit different now that Dad was no longer troubling the waitress. Surprisingly, Craig would give her a hard time, perhaps in homage to Dad.

It proved a lively affair and Dad was paying attention. There came a time when Craig got too excited and spoke too fast. Dad seized the opportunity and play mocked him with his old gibberish: "ooba dabba dooba dabba." And I repeated the gibberish without missing a beat—just as I used to do. We all smiled at each other. For one shining moment our family was the way it used to be. I thought, Dad's still in there. His general nature remains, although the edges are smoothed out. He's still fun to be with. He's still our dad. Only his memories and capabilities are impaired.

June 19, 2010 Kevin picking us all up at the airport to return Dad home - for the last time.

That night we stayed up late talking. It was nice having as much of our family around. Dad had his master bedroom, Kevin and Linda had a bedroom, and Craig and I shared the last bedroom. I take great pride in that I actually out-snored Craig—a not inconsiderable accomplishment as he's been known to keep awake entire campgrounds. I woke up fresh as a daisy. Craig looked like hell, and blamed it on me. His wife might ask where Craig got the nerve to complain about anyone's snoring, but there you have it. If it's any consolation, Craig, my sleep is usually crap. Probably was that night too.

Dad stayed up fairly late but he did go to bed before us. We took the opportunity to discuss the plans for taking him to the Arden Courts home. As sad as it was, our beliefs had only hardened that this was the best, and only, thing for him. He could not live alone and his time at Craig's proved that he would not live with any of us. The trick was how to get him to leave his home. Kevin and Linda had discussed this with the Arden Courts management. We all wanted to avoid a similar situation as when my parents had to drop off Dad's mother at a nursing home on the Cape. She had been losing her sense of reality due to dementia. Although she had periods of normalcy, the uncertainty of her episodes and the danger to herself meant that she needed full time care. Somehow Mom and Dad convinced her to go with them to a nursing home and management gave them all an introductory tour. Many of the guests were extremely old and infirm. They looked every bit their ages. When Mom and Dad started to leave, Nana, who unfortunately was in one of her alert phases, expressed her shock saying: "You're not leaving me here are you? ... With these goons?" It was a tearful goodbye as Mom and Dad drove away - alone.

Arden Courts counseled that the best way to get Alzheimer's patients to long term care was for the family to use a little subterfuge. Rather than risk a big argument over whether they need to leave their homes, families should let the patients think that the move is temporary - rather than the permanent stay that it is. Unbeknownst to Dad, we should pack a bag of clothing and essentials and sneak it out to the car to bring with us. Once inside, the director would greet us all and start a tour – with Dad as the focus of his attention. Kevin and Linda would hang back to transfer Dad's bags to his room. Craig and I would join Dad on the tour where we would peel off at some opportune time. That was the hardest part of the plan because it seemed like we were deserting him. But we were advised that in the Alzheimer patient's semi-confused condition with periodical brain resets, our departures would not be seen as unusual. (Talk about a leap of faith.) Between the newness of the facility and introducing Dad to the various staff and other patients, he wouldn't even notice our departure. At that time, Arden Courts would transition him gently to his new home.

But we needed to develop a story that would convince Dad to make the initial visit. The scenario that Kevin and Linda came up with was that we had scheduled repairs to the condo in preparation for sale. After all, Mom was dead. And the place was too big for one person. A maintenance crew was arriving early Monday morning to fix the plumbing. They needed to replace the main water valve, the sink supply valves, and the faucets for both the sink and shower. This required the potable water to be secured, possibly for two days. In addition, technicians were coming in to repair the Air Conditioning. The extent of repairs mandated that no one could stay in the house. We would all have to vacate on Sunday so that there would be no delay. A realtor had been hired who was going to oversee the repairs and afterwards assess the value of the property. Since Kevin and Linda have to work and David and Craig have reservations to fly home, we need to find a good place for Dad to stay for a few days. The place we came up with was Arden Courts. If necessary, we would be prepared to say that Mum had picked out the location before she went into the hospital. We all would visit and have lunch there.

Arden Courts would approve the plan. It was complicated though. I had difficulty following it myself. (This is a "condensed" version.) And I wondered if Dad would understand enough for it to work.

Sunday morning, Father's Day, we woke up and had a leisurely continental breakfast. Everyone was decompressing from last night's talks and it seemed like the calm before the storm. Dad was in his pajamas. We all sat in the living room talking and delaying as long as possible playing this necessary trickery on Dad. I was happy to take a subordinate role knowing that Kevin would do what was necessary. But this was difficult for him too, and he delayed longer than planned. Finally he marshaled his thoughts and put the plan in front of Dad.

June 20, 2010

While Kevin talked, I had conflicting emotions. Part of me was rooting for Dad to be the Dad of old: to see through the fairy tale of repairs, to spot the inconsistencies, to ask for alternatives. The other part of me wanted him to cooperate calmly because it was best for him—and easiest for us. I have to admit, Kevin was masterful. Dad listened attentively—and noncommittally. We all nodded and supported the story, acting as though we needed to leave immediately. Now was the moment of truth. Kevin offered that Dad needed to get dressed so that we could all leave. Dad wavered. Was he going to argue? Get defensive? Just sit there? It got a little tense but... we out waited him. Dad meekly got up, walked into his bedroom (for the last time), and started getting dressed. I felt so sad for him—as if he was giving up. But in reality, I don't think he could grasp what was going on. It was very difficult for all of us to watch this play out.

After Dad dressed and we were milling around gathering our own bags, we still continued talking about Arden Courts. We told Dad that he'd like it because it was a fancy hotel. What separated it from others was the level of service. They had many attendants who saw after the guests' every need. This was to prepare Dad for the personal attention he was going to get. With this positive enlightenment Craig and I got in Dad's car with him (Craig driving) and Kevin and Linda got in their car— with a bag or two for Dad secreted away in the trunk.

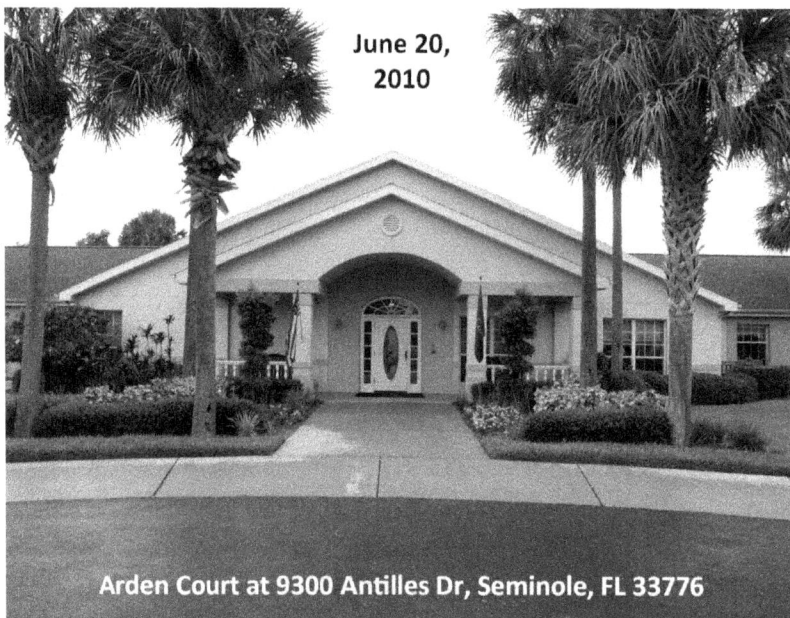

June 20, 2010

Arden Court at 9300 Antilles Dr, Seminole, FL 33776

The drive took close to an hour from New Port Richey to Arden Courts in St Petersburg. We all got out and walked to the foyer. The first "service" I noticed was the security. The door was locked via electronic controls. One couldn't get in – or out – without being buzzed from the receptionist station. Andrew Defosses, the Executive Director arrived in short order and welcomed us warmly. As promised, Dad was the center of attention, but Craig and I were very interested too because we hadn't seen the place yet. Andrew had warned us previously that the day we dropped Dad off would be very emotional and difficult, but more so for us than for Dad. We should console ourselves with this thought.

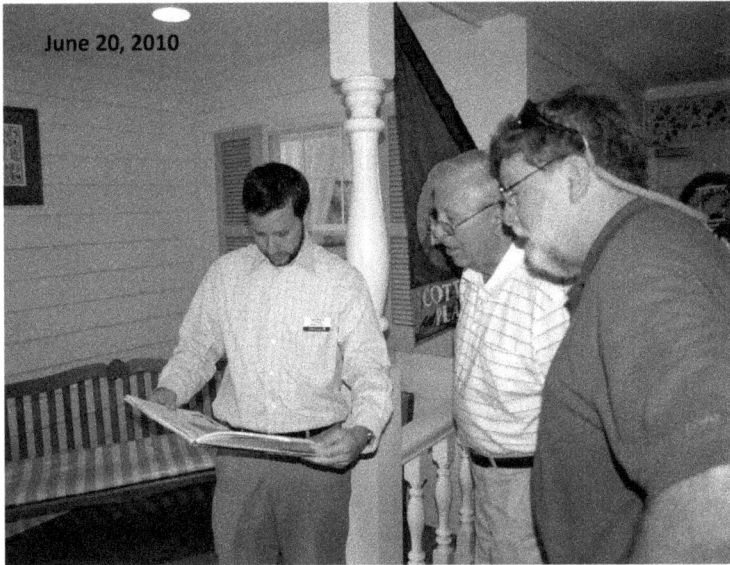

June 20, 2010

Kevin and Dad listening to Director Andrew Defosses at Arden Court

June 20, 2010

Dad with Kevin's wife, Linda, walking through Arden Court

We walked through the whole facility. Kevin and Linda stayed behind (to care for Dad's bags) but Dad didn't seem to notice. So far so good. And far from being upset, my emotions were very much in check. Maybe this wouldn't be such a sad experience after all. I was taking it all in and asking questions. We passed Boat House Cove, Cottage Place, and the Library. There were many cubby holes with bench seats where guests were sitting contentedly. Everyone was clean and they were treated with respect.

June 10, 2010

**Mr. Defosses showing us the library
with Craig, Linda, Kevin, Dad**

I noticed they were "Quiet Ones" just like Dad. One of the female guests wanted to walk with us. Andrew paid her attention as though her coming with us was the most natural thing in the world. Everywhere we went, Andrew introduced Dad around. Sometimes there was just a nod of the head, other times there were handshakes. Once, Dad even kissed one lady on the cheek. I got a good feeling for the place. These people would become Dad's new family.

At this point we reached Dad's room. There was a placard on the door welcoming Howard Williams. Kevin and Linda had hung a montage of family pictures too. Dad seemed pleased as he read his name and studied the pictures. I was as calm as could be at this point. Then Andrew opened the door and led us inside. It was like entering a new world for me. I went into emotional shock. My blood pressure pounded up. My sinuses closed. And my eyes started tearing. I could no longer talk. I felt barely human. Dad had lived a kingly life in comparison to this room that was his new home. Not only that but he had provided for others to live well too. His new room was a dorm room, sized for one occupant. There was no television, no phone, and no desk, just a small clothes bureau and a lamp. He did have his own half bathroom.

The door to Dad's room

Standing there rooted to the spot while Andrew talked to Dad about the accommodations, I remembered that the Arden Courts's philosophy was that the guests were encouraged to leave their rooms and socialize. The rooms are small on purpose. I agreed with it. But there was little that I could do to fight my body's reaction. In comparison, Dad accepted everything at face value. I shouldn't have been amazed, but I was. Again I was saddened because he couldn't comprehend enough to know that he should have been upset.

Andrew, Dad, Craig and I left the bedroom. I shuffled along at the rear, just putting one foot in front of the next, in a completely contrasting mood to when I entered the facility. We approached the kitchen and it was nearing time for lunch. Wasn't there something Craig and I were supposed to do? My cell phone rang in my pocket. Never liking those gizmos, I grasped it out. It was Kevin, "It's about time you guys peeled off and left Dad alone." Oh, that's right. The plan had gone out the window once I went into shock. I whispered to Craig. Then went up to Dad "I have to go to the bathroom." He just looked at me. I repeated it. Then I left. I felt like such a coward. Craig stayed behind. I don't know how he extricated himself but he joined me within a minute.

We joined up with Kevin and Linda in the lobby while Dad completed the tour and joined the other guests at lunch. My body was still in fight or flight mode and I knew that I needed some time off. I grunted something about going for a walk and went to the front door. It was locked. I took a couple steps back and someone buzzed me out. I stood outside the entrance letting my emotions wash over me, knowing that I couldn't talk to anyone at that time.

I contemplated the drop off proceedings. It's all geared for the guests. To keep them calm. To keep their stress levels down. And rightly so. To comply with this, we had to sacrifice our own feelings. There would be no goodbyes or any explanations. We wanted to cradle him in our arms, tell him we were sorry that he had to leave his home, tell him that we would love him and that we would take care of him. But he wouldn't have understood. His brain resets too frequently. Most likely our anxiety would have triggered confusion and anxiety in him. We would get no comforting closure.

After a short time, I thought I'd better rejoin everyone for the debriefing before we left. Staff arrived and I walked in with them. I still was unable to talk and used this opportunity to go the rest room to clear my sinuses and wash my face. When I returned, Andrew was giving some last minute advice for how long we should give dad before anyone visited. It usually took a couple weeks for guests to settle in. This was a particularly trying time for me as all I wanted to do was leave. Everyone else seemed pretty calm though. How is that possible? But maybe I appeared calm as well – and I knew that was anything but the truth. Finally we reached the end. I shook Andrew's hand, mumbled a thank you and left. I must have looked like an oaf. But that's all I could manage.

Departing the facility reminded me of the first time that I dropped off my infant son at day care. Could these people ever understand how important he is to us? Do they know how lucky they are to be with this fun loving fellow all day? The two situations are very similar. They are innocent and they trust us completely. What's different though is that I looked at Spencer and saw the intelligence in his eyes as he surveyed his surroundings, perhaps looking for me. A thought struck me then. He'll be ruling this place in three weeks. I couldn't get the same first feelings with Dad. He will only go downhill. But I do think that they are lucky to be with him. There's still a lot of live wire left.

That first week back I thought of Dad daily and I just imagine him re-questioning himself every half hour as to why he's there. Wondering what he should be doing. Asking himself who the caregivers are and who the other guests are. I wished that I could help him make the transition. They say that we shouldn't visit for several weeks to give him a chance to settle in. We telephoned for a status report. His first day he asked to go home. (This is common.) They told him that they were waiting for a cab and then redirected him until he forgot that he wanted to leave. He appears to be adjusting well. He seems to understand that he needs help and accepts it without complaint.

I am now home and contemplating the loss of (effectively) both parents. I felt a bit guilty that I wasn't more emotional when I received the news that Mom died. But taking care of Dad put those emotions on the back burner. Another week went by. It struck me that this is about the time that I'd telephone Mum. But she was no longer there. You don't appreciate your parents fully until they're gone and you realize that you've lost your most reliable sympathetic supporters. Did I appreciate her enough when she was alive? Probably not.

We grew up somewhat poor (especially by today's standards). Our first "permanent" house was a small three bedroom, one bathroom ranch (for seven of us) on the outskirts of town on a busy street in what was then called West Concord, MASS. We only had enough for essentials. Still Mom and Dad always made sure we had big birthday celebrations. And Christmas, and its lead up, was always the highlight of the year. We had the best childhoods imaginable. All thanks to Mom and Dad. You won't be forgotten.

Visits with Howard at Alzheimer's Facility

Kevin and Linda were under a great deal of family pressure to visit Dad at Arden Courts. Fortunately, they exercised restraint and followed this facility's instructions on permitting its caregivers several weeks to acclimatize him to his new life without any familial emotional interference. Over the phone we were told that, like most Alzheimer's patients, Dad frequently wanted to leave. He'd come up to the desk and demand a taxi. Interesting because it was doubtful he knew his address to find his way home. But the staff worked with him. They would tell him the taxi was on its way. When he complained what was taking so long, they'd offer that there was heavy traffic and it was taking longer than usual. This game of offering excuses would continue until the Alzheimer's kicked in, Dad forgot what he was doing, and they'd tell him that he was wanted at the next activity. After a couple weeks, Arden Courts became his home, and he stopped trying to leave. (Brilliant.)

Here's one of Kevin and Linda's first visits with Howard at Arden Courts.

Sunday, July 25, 2010 11:09 PM

Subject: Howard/Dad/Poppop is Doing Great!

Hi Guys,

Linda and I stopped in to see Dad/Poppop yesterday and he is doing great!

It looks like he has settled in very nicely over there in St Pete at the Arden Courts. We've been over to see him several times over the last month. Can you believe that he has only been there a little over a month - and he actually seems to be enjoying himself. He looked good, was clean and had a terrific attitude. He seems to be very content with his room, his new friends, and his surroundings.

We were a little concerned for the first couple of weeks or so that he would try to vacate the premises, but he has readily adapted to the daily regimen and he likes to participate in all of the daily activities - BBQs, singing, exercises, mingling, eating and etc. He is not interested in escaping – or "exit-seeking" as the caregivers call it.

When we first arrived at about 11:30 AM, he was in the activity room there with about 20 of the other residents listening to a briefing on the current newspaper events. (These are events/activities that are regularly scheduled for the residents throughout the day – everyday.) He appeared to be having a wonderful time – and we saw him chuckling and making snide remarks to the people around him – just like the Dad we know. He didn't see us through the shear window dressings.

We decided to let him continue with the briefing while we went to look into his room to see if there was anything he needed. To our surprise, we noticed Dad coming down the hallway with his arms outstretched with a big smile on his face. After the customary hugs, we proceeded to have a wonderful visit.

He has actually made quite a few friends there. Not only the caregiving staff, but also many of the residents on his wing of the building. In several of the pictures, you may notice a gentleman dressed in a dark blue shirt. He and Dad get along really well and are always joking around laughing. His name is Terry Gannon and we later found out that he was the Mayor of St. Pete Beach. We originally thought he might be a volunteer caregiver, but were astounded to find out that he is a resident! He certainly doesn't look that old.

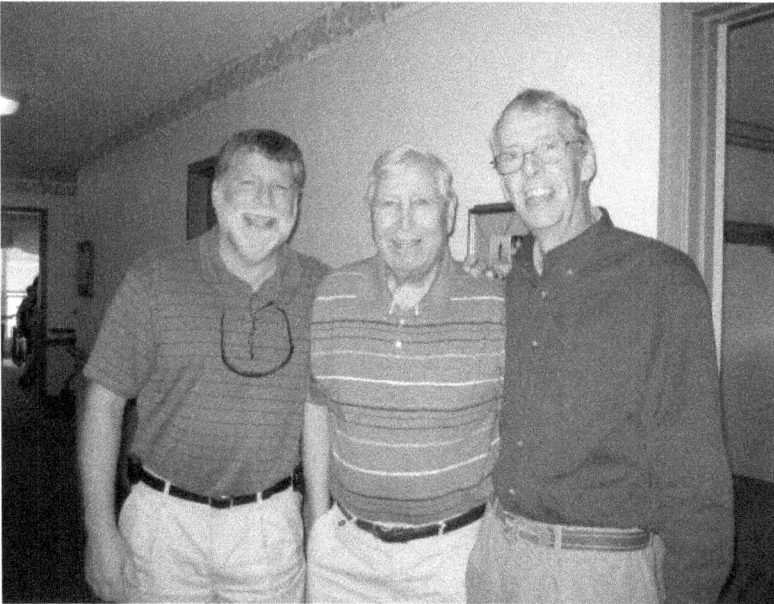

We took them both on a walk around the building and sat for a chat in one of several gazebos they have there. As you can see from some of the pictures, Dad was in a great mood.

It looks like we made the right choice with this place. Dad seems to be thriving with all of the attention, activities, and care that would have been difficult to provide in a residential setting. With his current attitude, it is going to be much easier for us to go over there in the near future. And anytime you guys want to come down and visit, we are sure he would love to see you.

We hope all is going well with everyone and maybe we can talk soon. We'll let you know how things go.

C'Ya,

Kevin & Linda

Here's a description of the activities offered at Arden Courts.

Arden Courts of Seminole Embraces a Culture of Engagement

Adult Engagement Therapy is a learning technique that uses familiar objects to retrieve once learned skills. We build on one step at a time, focusing on the *doing* of the task and not the completion. Success for the leader and the resident is found in the *doing* process; this is Engagement Therapy.

Program Descriptions

Religious Worship Service is led by Father Bob.
He gives a sermon and hymn singing. Residents can also receive Holy Communion. He is one our resident's favorite. Communion is given on Saturday morning from St. Jerome Catholic Church. Every Wednesday the Rosary is said by the Legion of Mary.

Devotions are daily in the mornings. Staff leader reads short happy stories from
"Chicken Soup for the Soul". Residents also participate in reading out loud as well. Hymn singing and ending with the Lord's Prayer.

Morning Moves is our routine exercise class. This is a structured physical fitness session that primarily focuses on stretching, breathing and toning of muscles.

Physical programs are usually group activities which improves self esteem and socializations. Bowling, Golf, Indoor softball, Basketball, Bean Bag Baseball, Bocci ball, Volleyball, Horse races and Nature walks.

Entertainment is scheduled throughout the month. Happy hour, ice cream socials, cheese and crackers are our Social parties.

Resident's Clubs involves different topics which is part of our **Engagement Therapy Treatment**. Here are some of our E.T.T* groups Ladies Conversation Club, Fitness Club, Art Class, Baker's Corner, Krafty Korner.
Family Nights are a time all families are invited to enjoy delicious food and great entertainment with their loved ones. Dance, eat and be merry, have a great time!!!

Brainstorming are games that use simple supplies to recall a skill once learned. Examples would be finishing quotes and rhymes. Reconizing photograghs of famous people & events from the past. This is *Enagenment Therpy*.
Helper's Corner are times that use simple tasks to recall a skill onced learned
folding laundry, slicing up fruit, cutting coupons and productive small tasks. Mixers are usually one on one or a small group program that focuses on the therapeutic value of participation. This is *Engagement Therapy*.

Resident Outings are every other month with residents voting on the outing of their choice. Residents have a monthly meeting in which they get to discuss where they would like to go on their outing. Outings are also a means of maintaining a connection to the outside world.

Creative Arts & Crafts offers residents an opportunity to express themselves through art. We have *Memories in the Making*, Alzheimer's Art Instructor aboard. Some of the showcased work from our facility is located on our Memory Wall.

Sing-a-Longs refers to singing hymns in the morning and nostalgic songs at other times. Sing-a-longs decrease agitation and other behavior problems. We encourage expression of feelings, especially through song and art.
Snack and Chat is an afternoon where we serve refreshments and try to stimulate group conversation by selecting a subject to discuss or just reminiscing. This gives the resident a chance to express their feelings and encourages socialization.

Engagement Therapy Treatment- Is a program for our early/mid stage Residents.
This is a smaller group program to encourage conversation & provide opportunities for meaningful events, encounters & exchanges with the person.
These programs are marked on the calendar with a star.** The Resident will receive an invitation to the club/program to make the even more special.

January 2011
Arden Courts of Seminole

Sun	Mon	Tue	Wed	Thu	Fri	Sat
Daily Program: 10:00 Morning Munch 10:30 Daily Devotions 11:30 Morning Moves 11:45 Newspaper Update		All programs are Engagement - Therapy Based. All Programs are Subject to change. E.T.T programs are Marked by a Star*				**1** 2:00 Boot Scootin Fran Show 3:30 Big Screen Show "Funniest Moments Of the Century" 4:30 Brainstorming 7:00 Lawrence Welk On Channel 3
2 2:00 Bean Bag Baseball 3:30 Afternoon Sing Along 4:15 Would you Rather/ Trivia 6:30 Evening Programs	**3** 9:40 Fitness Club* 11:00 *Ladies Gathering* 2:00 Indoor Softball 3:30 Afternoon Sing-along 4:15 Trivia Time 6:30 Evening Programs	**4** 11:00 *Ladies Conversation Club* 2:00 Steve's Jazzy Tunes 3:30 Afternoon Sing Along 4:15 Word Trivia 6:30 Evening Programs	**5** 9:40 Fitness Club* 11:00 Baker's Club* 2:00 Rosary Club/ I Love Lucy 3:30 Afternoon Sing Along 4:15 Mind Joggers 6:30 Evening Programs	**6** 11:00 *Ladies Conversation Club* 2:00 Eric's Piano Tunes 3:30 Afternoon Sing Along 4:15 Trivia Time 6:30 Evening Program	**7** 11:00 **Krafty Kroner'** 2:00 Music Madness 3:30 Big Screen Show 4:00 Resident's Pick 6:30 Evening Programs	**8** 2:00 Basketball Hoops 3:30 Afternoon Sing Along 4:15 Reminiscing Time 7:00 Lawrence Welk Channel 3
9 2:00 Ring Toss 3:30 Word Games 4:00 Afternoon Sing Along 6:30 Evening Programs	**10** 9:40 Fitness Club 11:00 *Ladies Gathering* 2:00 Drum w/ me! 3:30 Afternoon Sing Along 4:15 Reminiscing Corner	**11** 11:00 *Ladies Conversation Club* 2:00 Indoor Softball 3:30 Afternoon Sing Along 4:15 Mind Joggers 6:30 Evening Programs	**12** 9:40 Fitness Club* 11:00 Baker's Club* 2:00 Rosary Club/ Art Linkletter 3:30 Afternoon Sing Along 4:15 Word Games	**13** 11:00 *Ladies Conversation Club* 2:00 Eric's Piano Tunes 3:30 50's Sing Along 4:15 Word Trivia 6:30 Evening Pro-	**14** 11:00 **Krafty Kroner'** 2:00 Parish's Country Show 3:00 Ice cream social 3:30 Big Screen Movie 4:30 Residents	**15** 2:00 Indoor Softball 3:30 Afternoon Sing-Along 4:15 Trivia Time 7:00 Lawrence Welk On Channel 3
16 2:00 Bean Bag Flip 3:30 Afternoon Sing Along 4:15 Word Fun 6:30 Evening Programs	**17** 9:40 Fitness Club* 11:00 *Ladies Gathering* 2:00 Les's Ukulele Show 3:30 Sing-Along 4:15 Word Games 6:30 Evening Programs	**18** 10:15 Father Bob Church Service 11:00 *Ladies Conversation Club* 2:00 Bowling Match!! 3:30 Sing Along 4:15 ABC Trivia Games	**19** 9:40 Fitness Club* 2:00 Rosary Club/ Red Skelton 3:30 Afternoon Sing-Along 4:15 Word Games 6:30 Evening Programs	**20** 11:00 *Ladies Conversation Club* 2:00 Price is right! 3:30 Afternoon Sing Along 4:15 Winter Trivia 6:30 Evening Program	**21** 11:00 **Krafty Kroner'** 2:00 Larry Guitar Tunes 3:00 Ice cream social 3:15 Big Screen Movie 4:15 Residents Pick 6:30 Evening Pro-	**22** 2:00 Bean Bag Toss 3:30 50's Sing Along 4:00 Resident's Choice 7:00 Lawrence Welk On Channel 3
23 2:00 Ring Toss 3:30 Sing- Along 4:15 Reminiscing Corner 6:30 Evening Programs	**24** 9:40 Fitness Club* 11:00 *Ladies Gathering* 2:00 Indoor Softball 3:30 Afternoon Sing-Along 4:15 Word Games 6:30 Evening Programs	**25** 11:00 *Ladies Conversation Club* 2:00 Horse Races! 3:30 Afternoon Sing Along 4:15 Brainstorming 6:30 Evening program	**26** 9:40 Fitness Club* 11:00 Baker's Club* 2:00 Rosary Club/ The Lucy Show 3:30 Afternoon Sing Along 4:15 Word Games 6:30 Evening	**27** 11:00 *Ladies Conversation Club* 2:00 Bowling Match!! 3:30 Afternoon Sing Along 4:15 Word Games 6:30 Evening Program	**28** 11:00 **Krafty Kroner'** 2:00 The Earthlings 3:15 Big Screen Movie 4:15 Residents Pick 6:30 Evening Program	**29** 2:00 Indoor Softball 3:30 Afternoon Sing Along 4:00 Word Games 7:00 Lawrence Welk On Channel 3
30 2:00 Bean Bag Flip 3:30 50's Sing Along 4:15 Mind Joggers 6:30 Evening Program	**31** 9:40 Fitness Club* 11:00 *Ladies Gathering* 2:00 Price is right! 3:30 50's Sing Along 4:15 Reminiscing Corner 6:30 Evening Pro-					

David's e-mail of October 15, 2012

Hello all,

I just returned from Florida where my Clearwater High School graduating class of 1972 held their 40th reunion. Had a great time. There was a Friday evening happy hour, Saturday morning golf outing, and a Saturday evening dinner cruise. Eighty to 100 of us attended out of a class of 650.

I had no idea this would happen but I found that the people I knew (or knew of) are now a hundred times more interesting as adults. We're planning another outing in two years - to celebrate turning 60! I didn't know how much I missed Florida until this visit.

I also visited Dad at the Arden Courts Alzheimer's facility in Seminole. That's what I want to write about.

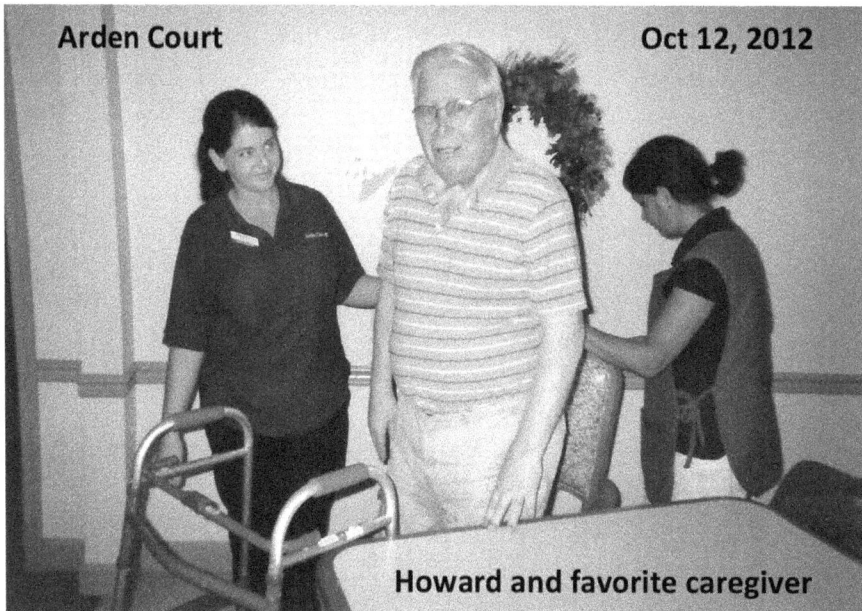

Arden Court   **Oct 12, 2012**

Howard and favorite caregiver

I arrived on Friday at 8:30 a.m., having read that dementia patients are more alert in the morning than in the evening. Seemed a good idea. The staff was very friendly and genuinely happy to receive visitors. This was even better, seeing as how I didn't give any advance notice. I wanted to make sure that they didn't have the opportunity to squirrel away any *Nurse Ratcheds*.

Dad had just gotten up and he and a dozen others were sitting in the dining area waiting breakfast. There were four or five tables that could seat four each. Dad was slumped in his chair asleep. So was the even older lady to his right. The lady on his other side was very lively and alert though, seemed to like Dad, and was very helpful to take care of everyone. I sat down next to Dad and one of the staff woke him for me. He didn't know me of course. But then I didn't expect him to.

Seeing him in the home was very difficult. I talked to him as best I could, but my body betrayed me - the same as it had when we had dropped him off over two years ago. Unbelievable. I thought I had it under control. But I got all choked up seeing him as he was, and it was difficult for me to talk.

He didn't look all that bad though. In fact he looked pretty good. He had gained a lot of weight early on at the facility but it looks like he's lost about half of that. What makes him look older is that he no longer dies his hair. No one else does either. Everyone's gray. It's too bad. They'd probably appreciate the attention.

Anyway, I knew it was crazy, but I couldn't stop my body's reactions. Seeing his general helplessness got to me. My blood pressure zoomed, my throat constricted, and my eyes watered. Haltingly, and talking in very short sentences, I showed him some pictures that I brought and explained who everyone was. He took an interest and offered comments: "Is that you? Who's this?" Although I explained that I was his son and he was my father, I don't think he understands what that means. Many of the other patients watched us and I couldn't help wondering what they thought of our chat - with me being so emotional and barely able to speak. (Some of them are lucid.) At one point I had to walk to the kitchen to get a glass of water. Just to get a break.

Fortunately, breakfast was served and I got a chance just to observe. They each got a small bowl of soupy oatmeal (not complaining), assorted bite size fruit, cream chipped beef on biscuit, and milk. I noticed that many of the people had to work at handling the forks and spoons. Dad too. He concentrated on his food to the exclusion of everything else. It was as though I weren't even there. There was one odd moment though when a caregiver reminded him to drink his milk. It was a full glass and I expected him to down it in several sips. But he put the glass to his lips and started drinking, and kept right on drinking, until it was all gone. When he finished he just sat there.

Dad's primary care giver throughout was a cute 30ish brunette, sporting some cleavage, and, surprisingly, some colorful tattooing down there. (Thanks to Johnny Syiek's emails, I notice these things.) This gal (I'll call her Lovie) is straight forward, lively, and wonderful with the patients. Dad is very fond of her. (At least I know where my taste in women comes from.)

After breakfast, the staff assembled the patients to return them to their rooms for cleanup and morning ablutions. As another male patient walked past, Dad reached out to shake his hand. They faced each other and Dad gave one of his patented tests of grip strength. (He's still in there somewhere.) Lovie got Dad his walker and helped him to stand up behind it. In rising, he leaned in to kiss her on the cheek. She noticed and leaned in too saying, "Oh Howard, a kiss. You must be in a good mood today." Continuing the assistance, she matter of factly told him that it looked like she'd need to change his pull-up because it looked like it needed it. "We'll go to your room to clean up."

Then Dad followed us out the door, through the passageway, and towards his room. Telling Lovie that I'd wait for them outside, I let him pass and watched from behind. Again, it was sad seeing him make his slow progress. There was a fullness in his pants that was hard to miss. As I considered this level of dependency I thought about his daily routine. He can't go anywhere without his walker. And he can't get his walker without help. That means that once put into bed, he's stuck there until someone comes. The staff must check on them periodically in the morning to see if they're awake and ready to get up. When they see their eyes open, they dress them and take them to breakfast. I waited in the hallway as Lovie changed him, cleaned him up, and redressed him. Dad's pretty good because he accepts this help willingly. He has a very cooperative and accepting disposition.

When they came out, I talked with Dad shortly before telling him that I needed to run an errand and then I'd come back later on. Because he didn't know who I was, I didn't feel comfortable hugging him, or even shaking his hand. So I touched his forearm and said my goodbyes.

Leaving Arden Courts, I drove to Dad's condo in New Port Richey to pick up his golf clubs so that I could play with my classmates on Saturday morning. I also wanted to leaf through any photo albums that might be there. I met Dad's neighbors Judy and Jim Baker who have a key to the flat and Judy let me in. I only expected to stay 45 minutes but there turned out to be way more albums than I expected. I was looking for one picture in particular where Dad and I had used a posthole digger to install the fence posts in the front yard of the McLean, VA house. Couldn't find it. But I only looked through half of what they have, so I retain some hope. I removed a couple of the albums and some loose pictures so that I can scan them in back at home. They had a lot of good stuff.

I drove back to Arden Courts to see Dad on my return to the Palm Pavilion Inn on Clearwater Beach. I wanted to catch him during some free time where I could ask him to show me around the place. But as luck would have it, I arrived at lunch time. Arghh! Fortunately, they had just cleared the plates. Armed with yet another photo album I sat down with him and we leafed through more pictures. Again, I don't think he understood that he was my father, or even knew what that meant. His whole world is pretty much Arden Courts and what is going on at that moment. I got the impression that maybe it was upsetting his routine that I was there. On two occasions, he looked up and said, "Are you still here?" It was just a tad upsetting that he would feel this way. I always felt that Dad and I shared a special relationship. We had many similar character traits (flaws?). And in his prime we really enjoyed one another's company. So sad. Those days are gone for us both, and forgotten for him.

I did find some entertainment during this second visit though. There was an old wheelchair bound lady sitting alone at a far table in the dining room. She started carrying on an old argument with someone (who wasn't there) she really despised. What was amazing was how clear her voice was. It was penetrating and she seemed to be making perfect sense as she said things like. "I want you to get the hell out of here. You're always sticking your big nose in everyone else's business." She sounded formidable. The staff told her on a couple occasions that the lady in question had left. But shortly thereafter each time she started up again. "I told you to get the hell out of here. You're always putting your hands on things that aren't yours—which is everything." Then she said, "I'm going to kill you all." I looked at her during these exchanges but she just sat in her wheelchair looking straight ahead—at nothing. It was incongruous because she looked so helpless and yet sounded so confident and in charge. Despite these alarming sentences, not a single patient took the slightest notice. Each was in his or her own world.

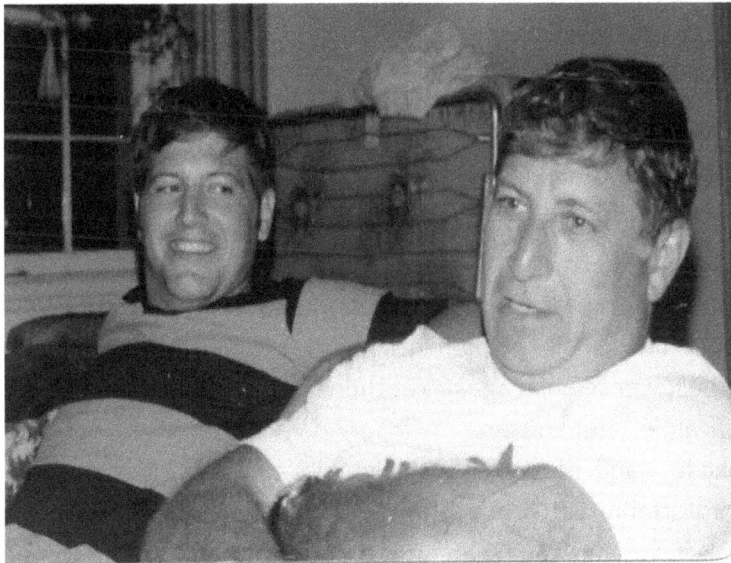

David (age 24) and Dad (50) Trip to Maine Oct 1978

Near the end of lunch, I asked one of the staff to take our picture, a close-up. I took out my comb and combed both our hair. He was slightly alarmed while I ministered to him but the staff told him it was all right. The picture taken, I noticed that Dad had given his usual dementia patient open-mouth look. For the next picture, I asked Dad to smile differently—something good that I could remember him by. There was some puzzlement and I explained that I wanted him to put his lips together. And I demonstrated myself. He didn't get it and seemed to get upset the more I asked him to smile differently. Finally I gave up and with Dad acting up, the woman snapped another picture. "This would be an 'action' picture," she said. From the picture you can see how uncomfortable Dad is because he's leaning so far away from me. It's sad; we used to be so close—see previous picture.

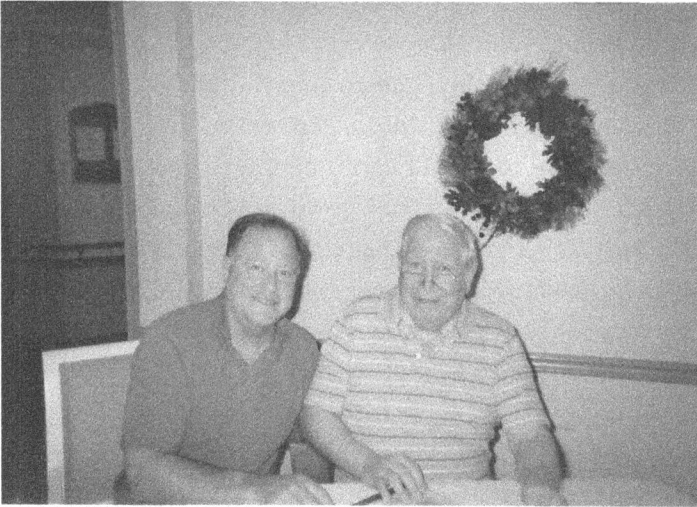

David and Howard at Arden Court, Seminole, Fl on Oct 12, 2012

After lunch, the staff announced that there would be entertainment in the activity room. They had a guitar player, a middle aged man, who was singing folk songs. Sounded pretty good too. The patients all were guided to the room and the entertainer sang as they were seated.

Despite never really having any close personal time with Dad, I felt that my visit was pretty much at an end. It struck me that when I left there was a good chance that I'd never see him again. Yet there was no way that he could attach a similar significance—not knowing me from Adam. Because of this I couldn't hug him or even shake his hand. I settled with giving him a goodbye pat on the arm as he settled in comfortably with his new family.

As I left, I thanked the staff and told them I thought they were doing a great job. (Much better than I could do as it turns out.)

Overall, considering the circumstances, I can see the bright side: Dad is comfortable, carefree, and happy.

David

****

I would never see Dad again as he would pass away suddenly during the night due to complications of ASCVD, Atherosclerotic cardiovascular disease. It was on February 1, 2013, an easy date to remember because it was only one day shy of dear Bruce's February 2nd birthday.

Memories of Pearl and Howard

For their 50th wedding anniversary in 2001, son Kevin and Linda organized a party and asked everyone who wished to write a "note to our parents congratulating them, possibly reminiscing when, where, and how you met, and maybe relating any fun stories and fond memories you had with them." Here they are, all dated June 9, 2001—their anniversary.

David's note: Reading these letters makes me wonder. You think you know someone really well, like your parents, and then you find out there's so much more that you didn't know. I'm grateful for all these letters.

From Linda Carter Williams, daughter-in-law

Dear Howard and Pearl,

Congratulations on your Golden Wedding Anniversary to the greatest in-laws I have!

Where do I begin with where we met for the first time? Of course—Kevin and I had travelled up to McLean, Virginia in the fall of 1983 to visit with you both. This would be the first time we met, even though Kevin and I had been dating since the fall of 1981. Sweet Pearl met us at the airport with a warm welcome of hugs and kisses. When we arrived at home in McLean, Howard was in his pajamas and robe, feeling a little out of kilter—maybe a little grumpy—after his nasal surgery. He was sporting a huge white bandage across his nose. That picture is engrained in my memory!

Your friends Earl and Eva Johnson were visiting, trying to cheer up Howard with a cake, decorated ever so delightful with a huge plastic proboscis. Howard did not seem too excited about his get-well gift. After the Johnsons left, we retired to the kitchen table—where important meetings took place—to discuss the surgery, wherein I tried to soothe Howard with a foot rub. How could I do that? I hardly knew you?

The next time we visited you in McLean, Kevin and I both wore our plastic nose glasses in the airport to greet you. Did you really recognize us right away? At first you decided to pretend not to know us. Then Howard, with a little smirk on his face, was making others stare at us. Why were you doing that? Didn't we look perfectly normal?

Pearl, the real experience with you particularly was translating your handwritten life stories into typed format for your famous book "The Adventures and Philosophies of an Old Lady" in 1996. Of course I found out quickly that editing was not an option—only spelling was allowed. Each and every comma was placed perfectly by you and was not to be moved or altered in any way. You also chose the photos carefully with precision for size and clarity. But I delighted each time I read and re-read your fun or touching stories and fond memories. Your book came out perfect! I love your book that we published together!

Thanksgiving—when we are able to get together—has been a special time with you. I love it when you come to stay over and Pearl cooks practically the whole meal—your moist baked turkey, mashed potatoes, turnips, your stuffing, and famous cole slaw. All I have to do is provide all the utensils, set the table, and open the canned whole cranberries. I love it!

Christmas

Christmas is another special time we have spent together at our home. It is a time we can relax and enjoy all the decorations, including the tiny lights, which Kevin has artfully put up all over the house, and his larger than life tree that he selected and somehow physically forced in the house. Sometimes we have opened presents on Christmas Eve, and sometimes we have waited to open all of them on Christmas morning—it was only a difference of tradition between us. Then on Christmas morning we are buried in wrapping paper, ribbons and bows, and presents when your family begins to call with Christmas greetings, and questions as to what they gave us and if we liked it. We always seem to panic a little when the phone rings. We always plan to write down a list of presents, so we would not be blank with short-term memory, but in all the excitement, we haven't been efficient enough yet for that.

Our adventurous trip to Stuart, FL on Easter weekend 2000 was also a memorable one. We stayed at Ed and Sally's beautiful condo on the St. Lucie River in Rio. The adventure started on Saturday when Howard left the condo by himself to attend Easter church services at the nearest Catholic church. He became listed as "missing" after about two hours—did he forget how to drive back to the condo?—so we sent a search party, namely Kevin and Sally, to find him. Consoling Pearl during their departure was not easy—she was convinced he was lost, driving around in circles, not knowing the phone number to call for directions. Sally returned with the message that they located Howard inside the church, calmly watching all the baby baptisms and confirmations that were scheduled that day. Kevin stayed at the church with Howard, so he could bring him back safe to the condo after he pried him away. Both appeared back at the condo safe and sound after several hours.

Our recent auto trip to Canada in August 2000 for a visit with Pearl's cousins, some of which she hadn't seen in 60 years, was lots of fun with you. It was magical to show you how close in driving time New Brunswick was from the Cape. We had a wonderful time visiting the relatives at each meal on each day. When we went to visit Shirley during the day, we had decided to eat lunch before we arrived for our visit, only to find out she had prepared a lovely lunch for us—namely ham sandwiches, pimento cheese sandwiches, and cookies for dessert. To be polite, we ate everything, and were quite full to the brim when we left, but we could only laugh at ourselves. Needless to say, we did not seem to want any supper that night. We had a delightful trip! And Howard, you are the one that mentioned to her cousins about this very important anniversary. I'm glad!

Pearl and Howard, I could go on and on with stories about our shopping sprees, or listening on the phone when you are discussing a situation fervently, or just watching humor unfold at every turn when I am around you both. It's definitely been fun!

Congratulations on your wonderful life together and many more years to come. And thank you for your son!

Love, Linda

Eva and Earl Johnson (near retirement age adult friends)

Dear Howard and Pearl,

Congratulations on your fifty years of marriage.

Remember when we first me? We both purchased a condo unit at the Rotunda in McLean, VA. When all the units were sold, the builder gave a beautiful brunch for all the owners. We met you two visiting with a neighbor of ours. You came up to look at our condo unit to see what furniture looked like in a unit similar to yours.

Later on you called from the gate, saying, "the Williams' are here to visit us." I said, "Who? Who are the Williams?" Since then we became special friends. We went out every Friday evening and had dinner. Then we took turns playing cards in our homes.

We had many, many happy times. Remember when we were playing "O hell" (you first dealt one card face up on your forehead and you don't get to look at your own card) David came in and there we all sat holding a card on our heads and laughing like crazy people. That was the first time we met David! In time we met all your fine sons.

You told us how you did when you put five little sons to bed, then you put your feet up and ate oranges. You also told us about the time you all ate a big pot of chile, and then you took an automobile trip!! Windows up & windows down!

Love to special friends,

Eva & Earl

Louis Glinos (Howard's oldest childhood friend—Uncle Louis to the five boys)

Howard and I grew up in Dorchester (Boston neighborhood) about ½ blocks from each other. We went to the same grammar school and played tackle football in the school yard that had the only good grass around. We always tried to get Howard on our side because he was "heavier" than the rest of us. I guess Mrs. Williams fed him very well.

During the winter we use to go sledding on a local "hill." Today it would be classified as a long mound. Howard had this humongous sled that was about 4 feet above the ground, and when he came down after you, to slew you, you could hear the runners thundering down the hill, and we would race for our lives.

The thing about Howard was that we always tried to get him to be on our side because he seemed to be able to hit the ball farther, run faster, and catch better than most of us.

His next door neighbors were the Hirtles. Mr. Hirtle was the quintessential Nova Scotia strong man. He worked as an iceman and had muscles coming out of his earlobes. He would sit on his front porch in his white muscle shirt, and watch over us.

One day that will live in infamy, Howard brazenly walked by Mr. Hirtle, and yelled, "Hirtle the turtle." Suddenly like a flash, Mr. Hirtle leaped over the front porch railing and the metal fence, and came streaming after Howard. He grabbed poor Howard by the scruff of the neck and held him up while Howard's legs were still moving. Howard never forgot that experience, ever.

We played a game of tag that involved having to stay on wood if you were not "it." Howard carried a piece of wood with him so he could put it on the ground and jump from it to a wooden fence.

During WWII, my mother did not like my hanging around with Howard because she said his father could be a German spy.

On Saturdays we would go to the movies for 5 cents, and then with another nickel, we would buy Canada mints. Howard's hero was the movie star Zorro. He wanted to wear his black nylon cape out to play, but Mrs. Williams prohibited it for fear Howard would really get too into the part.

As far as I can remember, Howard had no love affairs while living in Dorchester. However, things would change for the better when he moved to Osterville. I would get invited down for the weekend, and I'd take the train to West Barnstable. There I would be picked up in Mrs. Williams' green Hornet, AKA Nash. Later, I was soon to be riding in Mrs. Williams' '39 Grey Plymouth.

When I first visited Osterville, I was dumbstruck by all the people playing golf and sailing in their big sailboats. I returned to Dorchester and told my friends that I had indeed crashed into high society. But did they believe me? Of course not.

Howard had a good job of being lifeguard at Joshua's pond saving all the local "yutes" from drowning. I would take my inner tube and reader's digest and float around the pond getting waterlogged while I increased my word power.

Pearl Marney: Howard named her the "Pearl of Osterville." And he was immediately smitten when she wore her famous GREEN SHORTS. Mrs. Williams would make tomato and lettuce sandwiches on white bread for us. But that not being hearty enough, we'd go in and stare in at Pearl's kitchen window hoping to receive some tidbits. Mrs. Marney never weakened, alas and alack.

During my stay with Howard for the weekend, he'd fix me up with a date. Most memorable was Kathy Palches, the minister's daughter. She was a looker and if I had known how to kidnap her, I would have! We often went sailing in Howard's boat, the four of us. Remember what happened one night when we became becalmed, Howard???

The Millhill club in hy-bananas (as Howard liked to call Hyannis) was one of our favorite places to go dancing. And Pearl always drank CC & Ginger. Howard would ask for Ovaltine, but the waiter didn't know what it was. Howard said he was in training, but we never found out what for.

During two summers while I was in college, I got a job on the Barnstable police force, thanks to the intercession of Howard's uncle Mutt McGoff. With that job, I thought I had died and gone to Heaven. To the dismay of Chief Hinkley, I always carried my sidearm unloaded. He would ask, "Jeez, where are your shells?" "I have them here in my pocket Chief." What would I do, shoot the tires out from someone who might have been zipping out from the Foxhole?

Over the many long years, my family and the family of Howard and the Pearl of Osterville have remained fast friends (I'm faster than Howard now). But Howard drives around in an old faded Cadillac which Pearl says is good enough for him, and he sees me pulling up to his driveway in my "statement car."

He is so envious that I have not aged as much as he has, especially since he can't remember the name of the Japanese cook who use to cook up chop suey at the olde Uphams Corner market until the Japs attacked Pearl Harbor—and he disappeared.

So Pearl and Howard, even though I use to use a lot of ZnO for my lips that you kidded me about, Peaches and I still remained good friends while we hung out at the pond.

The end (at last.............)

Louis

Joseph Syiek (oldest childhood friend of Pearl and Howard's older kids)

I remember most about Howard and Pearl the open home and family they created, the ease and tease with which "outsiders" were accepted and targeted for mirth and laughter. The way they let us become one of their kids while theirs became part of our own family, yet kept a proper distance—both open and aloof. It seems like we got the better deal, subjected to a few humiliating barbs in exchange for hours of free play while their own sons joined us in hours of quarry duty in exchange for a few hours of fun.

Some snippets of memories: Engineer turned attorney, Belly laughs and BAD haircuts, Church and trick Sunday School lessons, Fort out back and Ice tea in the fridge, Halloween parties with the Carlins & Ryans, Karate master, Osterville summers, Littered driveways and lots of nick knacks.

Hope you enjoyed the 50 years as much as we did!

Love, "Joey" Syiek

Janet (Williams) Bare (niece)

Moccasins and tomatoes. These are my first memories of Pearl and Howard. Auntie Pearl in the kitchen in pink short shorts, while sleeveless blouse and pink (or were they turquoise?) beaded leather moccasins offering to cut my hair. The tomatoes are not such a pretty picture! Uncle Howard grew a patch in the only sunlight of the whole yard in the rear of the Main Street Concord house. Somehow, rough housing, I smashed a few of his precious plants (you know how he loves a tomato!) and he was livid. Or at least I though he was. For the next fifteen years I thought he hated me!

That all changed when I arrived on their doorstep (1974) on route to Africa for a two year Peace Corp stay. My spirits were low—and they made me laugh for 24 hours straight. They gave me such a warm welcome and send off. It was just what I needed.

Over the years I've often wished I was their daughter and not just a niece. We've been better about keeping in touch of late and I treasure our relationship. They mean a great deal to me. Howard, your wonderful sense of humor and sound advice and Pearl, your affection and frank opinions that lend themselves to lively discussions, they delight me. I don't believe I've ever spent an unpleasant moment with you.

Auntie Pearl and Uncle Howard, I celebrate your fifty years together and wish you much love and joy in the years to come.

Your niece AND God Daughter, Janet Williams Bare, Los Alamos, NM

Henry Snyder (Pearl's brother-in-law and, Uncle Buddy to her children)

At the time of their wedding, I hadn't the pleasure of meeting with Howard and Pearl. I just got recently acquainted with Pauline and had only seen her a few times. She told me that her sister was getting married down on the Cape. I remember driving her to South Station in Boston so she could be there. I think that it was shortly after that, she asked me to drive her to the Cape. It was there that I met Howard and Pearl.

We would see each other on our occasional visits to the Cape, especially at Christmas. I believe that Howard was still attending college in Boston during that time.

Polly and I got married in April of 1953. By this time Howard had completed college and took a job at the Wright Aircraft Co. in New Jersey. My job at this time consisted of doing a lot of service work on machines that my company had built in the New York, Philadelphia area. When I would go on service calls, I would always take Polly along and would sometimes stay at the apartment that they had in Lodi, NJ. As things got better for them, they purchased a nice home in Ramsey, NJ. We visited them there, and by now there were three sons, all very close in age. Polly used to say to me, "I don't know how Pearl does it with all of those [cloth] diapers. I guess it all worked out anyway. I believe from there, they moved to Concord, MA. I remember that quite clearly.

When Howard had an accident with his Mercury, I bought a whole new front for it. Howard and I changed it on Saturday (try and get someone to do that today). Craig and Wayne came along at about that time. So the house had to be enlarged by finishing the cellar (I think that I did the wiring) to accommodate the new family members. At this time we visited back and forth quite often. I remember you kids learning to drive in the new 62 Chevy, as young as you were.

At this time Howard was going to law school and I was starting my business. It was not long after that that I had my first legal problem. I asked Howard to represent me. It was to collect a sizeable amount of money. I did not realize the kind of people that we were dealing with. It got pretty rough; I told him I felt we should drop the case. He said because it was one of his first cases, he was going to pursue it right to the end. He followed through and won the case, although it was not easy.

I then hired him to incorporate my company. The work he did is still in effect today.

Eventually, time moved on, and Howard decided to move into the computer business. At that time (late 60s) they were relatively new. He moved to Clearwater, FL and started the business. I do not know how he made out but I do remember in the end that he had these monstrous computers in the living room of his beautiful home.

I guess that he decided to get his job back and move up north. He stayed at my house in Lynn, while Pearl was in Florida selling their house. I think from there they moved to McLean, Virginia where, if my memory's correct, stayed until both retired.

In 1985 Pauling met with an unknown accident in our condo in Ft Lauderdale and went into a coma. It lasted approximately 20 months. During that time Pearl flew to Boston many times to be with her. No one will ever know how grateful and thankful I was, and still am, for all her help.

After Pauline's death we drifted apart, but I always tried to keep in touch at least once a year at Christmastime. We also tried to get together once a year in Florida. This year our timing was off and we missed seeing them. We hope to see them next year. The summer time is a very busy time for us, but each summer both Betty and I keep saying that we should get up to the Cape to pay Howard and Pearl a visit, along with the Marney family. The time somehow slips by and before we know it the summer is over and we never make it to the Cape. Here again, we will see what happens this summer. I'd like to get together with Howard and see who has the grayest hair.

I feel that Howard and Pearl are two of the greatest and best friends I have ever had even though we are somewhat related.

These facts may not all be completely accurate, and are the best to my recollection; but being 76 years old my mind just isn't what it used to be.

I want to congratulate you both in your 50 years of marriage and hope that you have many more years that follow.

Congratulations, Henry and Betty

Edward Gallivan (former college classmate)

I was a classmate of Howie at Boston College for four years. We started in September 1948 with about 25 B.S. Math majors. Of the original group, 16 completed their Math Degree requirements. With such a small group and with everybody taking the same core and most elective courses, we all became pretty good friends and many of us have kept in touch through the years, even though we were separated by many miles.

As everybody knows, Howie laughs easily and when he begins to laugh it is contagious and very quickly everyone around him is also laughing. Howie can find humor in almost any situation. What a great way to be!

One time though it got Howie and most of his classmates in a little bit of trouble. It was our sophomore year and in our first English class of the semester our professor was introducing himself to the class and started to write his name on the blackboard. He got as far as "ASS" when of course Howie began to laugh uproariously and of course the rest of the class immediately joined in. The professor, whose name was "ASSAD", wasn't too happy with the outbreak. I am sure that at the end of the semester Howie, as the instigator, got a grade 10 points less than he earned (maybe an 85 instead of a 95) and the rest of the class probably got 5 points less than we earned. It was worth it!

The first time I met Pearl was at their wedding 50 years ago and I remember it as a beautiful day. Even though I grew up in Boston I had never visited the Cape until their wedding. I guess I must have liked it since Peggy and I have been living here full time since my retirement in 199?.

BEST WISHES ON YOUR 50TH WEDDING ANNIVERSARY, PEARL AND HOWIE!

Love, Peggy and Ed

David Williams (3rd son)

Dear Mom and Dad,

I'll always remember...

I'll always remember that you, Mom, were free with your opinions yet held a genuine concern for people and social issues. You loved watching those Sunday morning political show——like the McLachlan Group or Evans and Novak. Thank God you sided with the Liberals! I know it would be safer to be quiet but, thanks to Mom, I tend to lean towards the outspoken—perhaps even being self-righteous and gossipy. The other direction though of listening too much and saying too little is offensive, if not untrusting. Many may admire a Gregory peck strong silent type role model. I find people like this unimaginative and boring. Without having to defend a position, they express disapproval and attempt to usurp the moral high ground by manner and body language alone. I'm glad I join right in most discussions, right or wrong, and can offer up my own point of view.

Dad tended to downplay controversial issues - not wanting to "stir the pot." Still he had a unique way of expressing himself. To him I owe a wry, if biting, sense of humor. He could condense the essence of issues down to a few choice words or nicknames. About our enormous self-important German neighbor—"Ein Shwine"! About the unusual, not right, high schooler who lived across the street—"Ig Foo!" Bruce could do the same thing. On Williams' sportsmanship, he said, "We're poor losers...AND WORSE WINNERS!" Perhaps the best one was after arguing with Mom, Dad once said with exasperation to me, "Your mother doesn't have any opinions...Just Facts!!!"

Love, David

Jennifer Jane Clarkson (daughter-in-law)

When David and I were in the early years of our relationship, before wedded bliss and B.C. (before children), David and I went down a few times to McLean, VA to visit Pearl and Howard— a sort of getting to know you thing.

I can recall the first time I visited Pearl and Howard they had developed some preconceived notions about my social status (based on David's warped information, of course). One of the first things I remember Howard saying to me was, "I suppose your parents drive a Volvo." His face went from a "half-kidding Gotcha" expression to one of surprise when I said, "No, actually they drive a Chevy compact."

It seems that no matter how many times we visited their house, and how well I got to know them, Howard and Pearl could never remember my last name "Clarkson." For a long time, my family and I were referred to as the Harknesses—in the right "sound" ballpark, I guess. Well, finally, to make it easier to remember my name, Howard came up with an elaborate memory jogger. He would say, "Let's see, Superman, phone booth, Clark Kent... Ahh!—Kentson!" Nice try, Howard.

It's funny— now when we drive to Cape Cod to visit them, we always pass a sign for Harkness State Park, and I am reminded all over again.

Pearl and Howard, you have always been very warm and welcoming to me and to my family. Thank you! You are a wonderful and unique pair, and I know we all share some very happy memories of times in your company. My very, very best wishes for a happy 50th, and here's to many more happy years together.

Your daughter-in-law,

Jennifer Harkness Kentson Clarkson

Mandy Williams (daughter-in-law)

Pearl & Howard,

Congratulations on your 50th anniversary. Craig and I really look up to the both of you and hope one day we will be celebrating our 50th.

It seems like not long ago Chrissy was born (hard to believe 17 years). I have never forgotten the help you both gave us in raising her. You both gave us the foundation to become good parents. I remember how upset Chrissy was that we were moving out. I remember her telling me that she would come and visit Craig and I! After a lot of talking, she finally decided to live with us.

Every time she got mad at me or Craig, she would tell us she was running away to Grammy and Poppop's house. She'd go into her room and call you on the phone (pretty smart for a two and a half year old). While she was waiting for one of you to pick her up, she would pack her bag. The only thing she would put in it was her Knee-knee (blanket), then she would grab Kimmy (doll), and wait by the door. After a couple of hours, you would bring her home. She never remembered what she was upset about.

Not long after that we had Michael. Michael loved to go visit you both. I remember how excited he would get every time I mentioned Grammy and Poppop. Over the years Chrissy looked forward to Thursdays with you. Soon Michael would be old enough to go to McDonalds too. I think out of all of us I looked forward to all the down time most, even though I still babysat other kids.

I could go on telling hundreds of other stories, but I would have to write a book. The thing I remember the most is your kindness as parents, friends, grandparents, and in-laws. Thank You would never say enough for everything you've given us (but maybe if keep saying thank you, it'll add up). The both of you will always be special to me and I love you both.

Love,
Mandy

And now, a poem from me to you.

Pearl & Howard you will always have a special place in my heart.

50 years of love,
And devotion.
Has its days,
Filled with commotion.

5 boys to raise,
A job to keep.
The housework would never,
Seem complete.

The laughter, the tears,
That once filled our home.
Seem to be fading with,
All of them grown.

All of our memories,
We have to share.
This is an important part,
Of our daily care.

New memories are growing,
Day-by-day.
6 grand kids later,
To show the way.
The gatherings, the reunions,
All filled with love.
You both made this possible
With God above.

Your love and guidance,
Got us here today.
That's why we all owe you,
In our own special way.

Christina Marie Williams (grandchild)

Congratulations Grammy and Poppop!

You've finally made it to your golden anniversary, that's fifty years of love and devotion to not only each other, but the rest of the family as well. If you think about it, that's about three times the amount of the time I've been alive. Seventeen years ago, when I first was born I came to live with you guys [in the finished basement]. I was your first grandchild, and was the only grandchild lucky enough to be able to live with you. As a little girl, you guys bought me some of my favorite possessions (knee-knee, Kimmy, and Teddy Ruxpin) all of which I still have.

While I lived with you, you both always made time to spend with me. When I was finally old enough to walk, I would bang on the basement door every morning and yell the famous phrase "opa door." And every morning one of you guys would come get me and bring me upstairs into your bed. You both always had extra time for me. Some of the best childhood memories I have are from when we used to play school, ride our bikes around the church and popping the acorns down by the church. I remember when we used to play school, Grammy always used to get to be the principal. Poppop and I used to have so much fun, going really fast when we used to ride around the hill at the church. It's really unbelievable how we never got bored riding up and down the same hill, just about every day. And even after we got tired of riding up and down the hill, sometimes we would ride our bikes around at the bottom of the hill trying to see who could pop more acorns.

While I was out on the back patio one da y, I saw a "nake" (snake), all I could think to do was scream. All I had to do was scream, and Poppop came to the rescue with his heroic capabilities, to save me from the "nake." Even after I grew up some and moved out we still spent time together. Every Thursday we would go to McDonald's, but it wasn't just about going to dinner, it was our reserved evening to

spend time together. Even now that you guys don't live in Virginia anymore, I have come to visit you each and every summer. And every time I come to your house, I still have an enjoyable vacation. It takes a lot of time, and effort to be as great of grandparents as you both are. You guys are obviously very dedicated to your family, and I really appreciate all the time and effort you've put into helping me to become the person I am.

Love, Chrissy

Michael Hank Williams (grandchild)

Dear Grammy & Poppop,

Congratulations on your 50th
I remember when I was very little and we use to go to McDonald's every Thursday. After McDonald's we would go to CVS and get a toy. I always used to want

those handcuffs. I also remember playing howdos (cars) and golf. We used to have so much fun every summer when I came to the Cape to visit you guys. Joshua's Pond will always be one of my fondest memories from the Cape. We always played croquet and sat down to feast on lobsters, and each time we still had an enjoyable time. Maybe when I get older I will be able to work on the Cape during the summer.

I just want to Thank You for being good Grandparents and giving me a lot of special memories.

Love, Michael
****

A week after the 50th anniversary and the guests had all departed for home, I (David) wrote this e-mail.

June 13, 2001

Dear Mom and Dad,

I can't tell you enough how much I enjoyed the celebration of your 50th wedding anniversary last weekend. Preparing for it caused me to remember far back to happy stress-free times. Then, reading from your "Keepsake Album" brought back even more fond memories. Even the impatient reception given to my perhaps overlong talk only dampened my spirits for a very short time. Now I think all the immediate feedback I got only added to the spirit of the occasion. I actually admired some of the humorous hecklings. I especially liked "Now we know why they don't let him talk" and "My anniversary is coming up soon. Please don't invite him."

I feel a little bit sorry for Kevin though. It really was his role to be the big wheel and address the crowd. He and Linda did almost all the organizing and prepared the Keepsake Album. At least Kevin presented you the Album and spoke to the immediate family. But early on I was offered an opportunity to thank everyone for coming and to say a few words to you in gratitude for raising us. Maybe I went too far and should have stuck to a ten-minute talk. Because afterwards, even if Kevin wanted to say something, the moment was gone. Live and learn.

The best part by far for me though was that we were all gathered together and were as close as possible to our original nuclear family of old. With the distances apart that we all live, sometimes I've felt that we were growing apart emotionally as well. It was great seeing that all the old loving feelings could return—and how natural it was for everyone.

While driving home I couldn't think of any way that this occasion could have been any better. Then I flushed thinking of Bruce and how much he would have truly enjoyed experiencing the loving feelings of old, the playful verbal jousts, and the laughter. I still had a great time but I knew then how it could have been better — much better.

Thanks for everything, David

Obituaries of Howard, and Pearl

Howard Winthrop Williams Obituary 2013

A personally religious, scrupulously honest, and caring man who was married for over 59 years, to Pearl (Marney) Williams, (deceased) of New Port Richey, FL and Osterville, MA, Howard, age 85, died suddenly from complications of ASCVD on Feb 1st. He and Pearl raised five children: Kevin, Orlando, FL; Bruce, deceased; David, Media, PA; Craig, Falls Church, VA; and Wayne, Hyannis, MA. Also surviving are six Williams' grandchildren: Christina, Michael, Rebecca, Jonathan, Spencer, and Oliver.

The deceased met his wife while they attended and graduated from Barnstable High School, Hyannis, MA, where Howard was the Senior Class President. During the early marriage, he completed a BS Math degree from Boston College (1952), a BSME degree from the New Jersey Institute of Technology (1956) and a Juris Doctor Law Degree from Boston College (1963). A licensed attorney he primarily worked as a Professional Engineer and retired in this capacity from the Mitre Corporation, McLean, VA in 1991.

Listing his engineering involvements would take pages. Here are a few of his early cutting edge DOD assignments from the 1950s and 1960s: conducted full-scale jet engine (YJ67) development tests and supersonic wind tunnel tests on high-Mach compressor blade configurations; conducted computer simulations of USAF century-series aircraft performance in SAGE System Air Defense environments; developed SAGE improvements in Radar Tracking and A/C Identification.

In retirement, the Williams' lived in New Port Richey but for slightly less than six months each year they resided on beloved Cape Cod, MA where they own a house in Osterville and are surrounded by Williams/Riedel and Marney relations.

An athlete in his youth, he maintained his competitive fire by taking up Karate in his 40s and achieved the rating of Black Belt. He also competed in some local Senior Olympics track and field competitions in the Washington DC area while in his 50s.

In retirement he enjoyed the daily routine of keeping up the houses, reading, sitting outside, entertaining family visitors, and playing golf. Other favorite hobbies included daily exercise, coin collecting, genealogy, personal videotaping of his family, and recording shows of interest from TV.

He will be remembered lovingly for his willingness to work and help, acceptance of others, ready laugh, and quick wit.

The family wishes to express their deepest appreciation to the Arden Courts Senior Care Facility of St Petersburg, Florida for being Howard's second family for the last two and a half years of his life.

Pearl Marney Williams Obituary 2010

WILLIAMS, Pearl Marney, age 83, passed away peacefully Tuesday, June 8, 2010, in New Port Richey, FL, where she will be cremated. She was born March 9, 1927, in Fairhaven, MA, the second daughter of the late Fraser A. Marney and Martha O. Parker, both of Osterville, MA. She is survived by her husband of 59 years, Howard W. Williams, of Osterville, MA and New Port Richey, FL.

Pearl grew up in Osterville and lived in many locations up and down the East Coast, including Concord, MA, Clearwater, FL, and McLean, VA, before retiring with her husband to New Port Richey, FL during the winter months with summers on the Cape.

She led a truly challenging and inspiring life that included being a loving mother of five boys, a credit manager for the Hecht Co. in McLean, VA, and eventual retirement from US Government Service at the CIA's Northwest Federal Credit Union. A talented self-taught poet and author, her works included several autobiographical books: The Adventures and Philosophies of an Old Lady and The Golden Years that Tarnished. She always regarded her childhood memories with fondness while growing up in Osterville on Cape Cod, and considered them the most rewarding experiences a child could ever have.

She was loved by all who knew her, and will be greatly missed by her family and friends. She was an amazing, strong-spirited, and compassionate woman, with an interesting point of view on just about anything, including politics and religion. She will be remembered as a loving wife, mother, grandmother, sister, cousin, aunt and friend who always enjoyed a good laugh.

Pearl is preceded in death by her sister, Pauline Marney Snyder, two of her brothers, Kenneth and Edison Marney, and one of her dear sons, Bruce Williams.

She is survived by two brothers, Osborne Marney of Centerville, and Arthur Marney of Osterville, MA; four sons: Kevin and wife Linda of Orlando, FL; David and wife Jennifer of Media, PA; Craig and wife Mandy of Falls Church, VA; Wayne and wife Bridget of Hyannis, MA; and six grandchildren: Christina, Michael, Rebecca, Jonathan, Spencer, and Oliver.

Pearl truly loved all of her family and friends, and wanted each to know that she would see them all again with the Lord in Heaven.

A celebration of life is planned in the coming future and will be announced.

In lieu of flowers, donations are requested to be sent in her memory to Hernando Pasco Hospice.

Memorial Service for Pearl and Howard

CELEBRATING
THE LIFE
OF
HOWARD & PEARL WILLIAMS

JUNE 29, 2013

10:00 a.m.

OUR LADY OF THE ASSUMPTION PARISH

OSTERVILLE, MA

Entrance Hymn
You Are Mine

Old Testament Reading
Ecclesiastes 3:1-12
Christina Williams

Responsorial Psalm
Shepherd Me, O God

New Testament Reading
Romans 14:7-12

———————————

Gospel Acclamation
Celtic Alleluia

Gospel
Luke 9:51-62

Homily
Fr. Mark Hession

Prayers of the Faithful
_____

Offertory Hymn
Precious Lord, Take My Hand

Presentation of the Gifts
_____

Communion Hymn
How Great Thou Art / Quão Grande És Tu

***
In lieu of eulogy, please reflect on the two poems
selected by David W. Williams.
(When I'm A Little Old Lady & Cranky Old Man)
***

Recessional Hymn
Eye Has Not Seen

This poem reminded me of the family part of Mom and Dad in raising five children. As a "Little Old Lady" mom never lived with us, nor felt the urge to "get even" with us - leastways not that I know of. But the poem does illustrate in a humorous way the trials of raising children and makes me appreciate more all the effort Mom and Dad made in raising us.

David

WHEN I'M A LITTLE OLD LADY

When I'm a little old lady

Then I'll live with my children and bring them great joy.
To repay all I've had from each girl and each boy

I shall draw on the walls and scuff up the floor;
Run in and out without closing the door.

I'll hide frogs in the pantry, socks under the bed.
Whenever they scold me, I'll hang my head.

I'll run and I'll romp, always fritter away
The time to be spent doing chores every day.

I'll pester my children when they are on the phone.
As long as they're busy I won't leave them alone.

Hide candy in closets, rocks in a drawer,
And never pick up my clothes from the floor.

I'll plead for allowance whenever I wish.

I'll stuff up the plumbing and deluge the floor.
As soon as they've mopped it, I'll flood it some more.

When they correct me, I'll lie down and cry,
Kicking and screaming, not a tear in my eye.

I'll take all their pencils and flashlights, and then
When they buy new ones, I'll take them again.

I'll spill glasses of milk to complete every meal,
Eat my banana and just drop the peel.

Put toys on the table, spill jam on the floor,
I'll break lots of dishes as though I was four.

What fun I shall have, what joy it will be to
Live with my children... the way they lived with me !!!

(author unknown)

This poem shows what happens to all of us if we live long enough. The title misleads though as Dad was never a "Cranky Old Man". Even as he struggled mentally, he retained his basic joviality. Dad enjoyed a full and rich family history that left a mark on his spirit that could not be erased even as his synapses faltered.

CRANKY OLD MAN

What do you see nurses? .... What do you see?
What are you thinking........ when you're looking at me?
A cranky old man, ... not very wise,
Uncertain of habit.......................... With faraway eyes?
Who dribbles his food....................and makes no reply.
When you say in a loud voice...........'I do wish you'd try!'
Who seems not to notice..........the things that you do.
And forever is losing...........................A sock or a shoe?
Who, resisting or not...................lets you do as you will,
With bathing and feeding...............The long day to fill?
Is that what you're thinking?.....Is that what you see?
Then open your eyes, nurse,......you're not looking at me.
I'll tell you who I am.........................As I sit here so still,
As I do at your bidding,......................as I eat at your will.
I'm a small child of Ten.........with a father and mother,
Brother and sisters...........................who love one another
A young boy of Sixteen...................with wings on his feet
Dreaming that soon now...........................a lover he'll meet.
A groom soon at Twenty...................my heart gives a leap.
Remembering, the vows...............that I promised to keep.
At Twenty-Five, now.....................I have young of my own.
Bound to each other...............With ties that should last.
At Forty, my young sons............have grown and are gone,

But my woman is beside me...............to see I don't mourn.
At Fifty, once more,...............Babies play 'round my knee,
Again, we know children....................My loved one and me.
Dark days are upon me.......................My wife is now dead.
I look at the future.........................I shudder with dread.
For my young are all rearing...............young of their own.
And I think of the years...And the love that I've known.
I'm now and old man...............................and nature is cruel.
It's jest to make old age...............................look like a fool.
The body, it crumbles...................grace and vigor, depart.
There is now a stone..................where I once had a heart.
But inside the old carcass...........A young man still dwells,
And now and again........................my battered heart swells
I remember the joys.........................I remember the pain.
And I'm loving and living................................life over again.
I think of the years, all too few..................gone too fast.
And accept the stark fact...............that nothing can last.
So open your eyes, people................................open and see.
Not a cranky old man..........Look closer.........see......ME !!!
(originally by Phyllis McCormack; adapted by Dave Griffith)

FAMILIES ARE FOREVER

Please keep us close together
And help us to be good
And always love each other
The way a family should.

When our lives are over
Please let us meet again
So we can be a family
Up in heaven, Lord.
Amen

(Author unknown)

**From Pearl's book
The Adventures and Philosophies of an Old Lady**

Immediately following:
All are welcome to a reception at the home of
Howard & Pearl Williams
77 Milne Road
Osterville, MA

Take right out of church onto Wianno Ave which becomes Main St.,
In .6 miles, turn right onto Pond Street
Turn left onto Milne Road
House is on your left

www.ingramcontent.com/pod-product-compliance
Lightning Source LLC
Chambersburg PA
CBHW050634150426

42811CB00052B/806